The Blended Family

SOURCEBOOK

A Guide to Negotiating Change

David S. Chedekel, Ed. D.
Karen G. O'Connell, Ph.D.

Contemporary Books

Chicago New York San Francisco Lisbon London Madrid Mexico City
Milan New Delhi San Juan Seoul Singapore Sydney Toronto

Library of Congress Cataloging-in-Publication Data

Chedekel, David.
    The blended family sourcebook : a guide to negotiating change / David
Chedekel and Karen O'Connell.
       p.   cm.
    Includes index.
    ISBN 0-7373-0387-5
    1. Stepfamilies—United States.   2. Remarriage—United States.
I. O'Connell, Karen, 1947– . II. Title.

HQ759.92 .C49   2001
306.85'0973—dc21   2001047584

Contemporary Books

A Division of The *McGraw·Hill* Companies

1 2 3 4 5 6 7 8 9 0 DOC/DOC 1 0 9 8 7 6 5 4 3 2

ISBN 0-7373-0387-5

This book was set in Sabon
Printed and bound by R. R. Donnelley—Crawfordsville

Cover design by Victor Perry
Cover photographs copyright © PhotoDisc
Interior design by Rattray Design

McGraw-Hill books are available at special quantity discounts to use as premiums and
sales promotions, or for use in corporate training programs. For more information, please
write to the Director of Special Sales, Professional Publishing, McGraw-Hill, Two Penn
Plaza, New York, NY 10121-2298. Or contact your local bookstore.

This book is printed on acid-free paper.

Contents

Preface

DURING OUR MANY years as valued colleagues and trusted friends, we have had several "what if" conversations about what former clients could and should have done in a more proactive way to prevent the stresses and strains that ultimately brought them to us for professional help. As a result of these speculations, we have written a book in an effort to encourage and enable proactive behavior and help those struggling with family changes to pace their transitions thoughtfully and cautiously. It is our hope that the examples we offer will assure families in transition that they are not alone and help them to understand that change—even positive change—does not come easily. Additionally, we hope that this book will serve as a reminder to readers that during each stage of the blending process they must take into account the needs and perspectives of everyone involved.

As society becomes more diverse and tolerant of diversity, the issues of blending families have become increasingly complicated. Families cross previous boundaries of race, religion, and sexual preference. And, as people delay marriage and childbearing, many find that their families include aging parents in their households. Some family units are formed without a traditional wedding. Because of these societal changes, the definition of family for the purposes of this book is a broad one: any unit of individuals, with or without kinship affiliation, who have committed to sharing their lives on a daily basis.

There is nothing that offers more comfort and security than the knowledge that you are part of a functional, loving family. Both of us had the good fortune to grow up in such an environment. We believe that solid background, in addition to our clinical and consultative experience with children and families, gives us real insight and understanding to help our readers find some guidance, support, and practical solutions to their blending dilemmas.

The examples we have chosen for this book illustrate the blending dilemmas we have encountered during our many years of working with families. However, all our case examples have been modified for the purpose of maintaining confidentiality. No actual names are used.

Acknowledgments

WE ARE GRATEFUL to Jack Artenstein for inviting us to pursue this project; to Maria Magallanes, our editor, for her patience, encouragement, and technical skill; and to Laura O'Hare, who made invaluable contributions to the development of this book. We extend our appreciation to Roger and Elaine Gardner for their willingness to manage our frenetic bicoastal communications, and to Kimberly Meaney for her timely research support. We also thank both our families, who were tolerant and supportive throughout this process. And finally, we would like to thank the people with whom we have had the privilege of working in our clinical practices. Without their courage and hard work, this would not have been possible.

1

Divisions That Lead to Blended Families

WHETHER IT'S IMMEDIATELY obvious or not, every family is blended. Anyone who's ever been to a family gathering knows that being part of the same gene pool is no guarantee that people share the same values and beliefs or even have the simple ability to get along. The born-again son in a family of atheists, the liberal Democratic daughter who hails from a long line of staunch Republicans, the gay uncle or bohemian cousin in a traditional midwestern family, the drinker in a family of teetotalers, the vegetarian progeny of cattle ranchers—even members of an immediate family can have great differences to deal with.

The blended family issues in this book involve dissolution of and addition to the immediate nuclear family. Parents divorce and find new partners, a same-sex couple decides to adopt a child, the long-married parents of teenagers bring an ailing parent into the family home—shifts in the traditional nuclear family are made every day. Yet no matter how often they occur, not only are these choices never easy, they are generally extraordinarily painful and traumatic.

Often, the process of blending a family is precipitated by loss— most commonly divorce or death. Therefore, we begin this book with a chapter on endings. For those who are in the midst of dealing with these issues, this chapter can help you navigate your way through this stressful experience. For those dealing with the ramifications of these events some time after their occurrence, this chapter is not about "what ifs" but about "what will be"—a means to understanding what went wrong and how it may still go very right.

Divorce

According to the National Center for Health Statistics, the arm of the Department of Health and Human Services that collects data on marriage and divorce in the United States, the divorce rate (per 1,000 population) has climbed from a low of 0.7 in 1900 to a high of 5.3 in 1981. The most currently available statistics indicate a slow decline since the early eighties. The rate in 1999 was 4.1. Yet, this drop does not necessarily mean people are doing a better job of maintaining traditional family systems. This drop has clearly been influenced by the numbers of people who have chosen to live together without marriage.

Divorce is generally defined as the dissolution of a marital partnership. Those who have been through it know it affects far more people than just the marital partners—it affects children, in-laws, friends, and extended family members. The ramifications are both emotional and economic, and they can be lasting, particularly if you have children. Although feelings and tempers are understandably volatile while contemplating and participating in a divorce action, the more you consider the long-term consequences of your decisions and behavior, the better off you'll be.

Preparing for Divorce

Becoming informed before beginning divorce proceedings will help make the procedure less difficult. It's crucial to collect as much varied information as possible—don't follow a course of action simply because it worked for a friend or colleague. Every situation is different. This is the time to think and plan carefully. Put hurt feelings aside as much as possible to fairly and reasonably assess what you hope to accomplish.

Clearly, divorce is a major life change and one that affects economics as well as emotions. It should not be undertaken without professional advice from a solid matrimonial lawyer. The immediate expense of a good attorney will pay off in the long run, as the long-term costs resulting from poorly executed divorce settlements can be enormous in terms of finances, emotional health, and family relations.

That said, all attorneys are *not* created equal, nor is a hefty retainer a guarantee of first-rate representation. Two things are vital when looking for the best attorney for you. First, interview a few. Take your time—haste can result in great waste—both of time and finances. Find out the attorney's history and try to ascertain if his or her approach is right for you. Does he or she work toward the most amicable divorce possible? Or is it his or her solitary purpose to obtain the greatest share of the marital assets, no matter the emotional cost? The first choice is probably best if you're sharing custody of toddlers with an ex-spouse you can get along with but no longer want to live with; the second is a necessity if you discover your once-better half has taken all the family assets and deposited them in an offshore account. Ask yourself if you feel comfortable talking to the attorney. Is he or she respectful (answering your questions easily and with respect for your intelligence) or patronizing (dismissing your questions by suggesting you simply trust him or her to take care of everything)? If another client is willing to talk to you, find out if he or she feels adequately represented— were his or her needs, not to mention telephone calls, responded to? Also, call the local branch of the bar association and take a trip to the local courthouse to find out what you can about your potential attorney's reputation. The last thing you need is a lawyer whose very presence is going to alienate half the judges in your municipality.

Second, remember who's in charge. Your attorney knows things you don't, but he or she still works for you. Don't let your attorney make decisions against your better judgment simply because he or she's the expert. Remember, as conscientious as the lawyer may be, you're still one of many clients from whom he or she's going to accept payment and move on. You are the one who is about to make choices that will affect the rest of your life. The more involved you are when it comes to your case, the better you'll feel in the long run. Think of it this way: it's one thing to make a decision from the heart that turns out perhaps not to be the best one. Everyone makes mistakes and moves on. However, if you do something against your better judgment that turns bad in the long run (just as your gut told you it would), it can result in a lifetime of often-debilitating regret.

Once you have begun to be clear about your emotional and financial goals, you will have to factor in the inevitability of sacrifice and compromise on the part of both you and your soon-to-be-former spouse. For one thing, the income you have been accustomed to as a family will now be supporting two separate households. It is unrealistic not to expect your lifestyle to change.

This leads us to the biggest issues in divorce cases: hurt feelings, anger, and hostility. When children are involved, this emotional minefield can be disastrous. Even in the most difficult situations, it is truly in your and their best interest to maintain as much as possible civil and consistent communication in regard to their welfare. The more you can avoid using financial issues to punish or exact retribution in the short term, the better things will be in the long term. Remember, the biggest winner in small financial battles is generally the attorney.

Professionals Who Can Assist You with the Issues of Divorce

There are, of course, a variety of issues involved in divorce, and you may need the help of different professionals to deal with those issues in the best way possible.

Mediators

One means of achieving a civil level of discourse is mediation. For mediation to be successful, however, both parties must be willing to work together cooperatively and fairly in an effort to resolve disputed issues. For the same reasons, mediation would likely not be helpful in a situation involving abuse, drug or alcohol dependency, or even one partner's extreme unwillingness to let go. The notion that cooperation, rather than opposition, is the way to achieve dispute resolution is the key to a successfully mediated divorce.

There are some real advantages to mediation as opposed to the courtroom. A mediator is a neutral third party trained in problem solving; he or she is not an attorney. Mediation can offer the parties real control over important decisions rather than ceding those decisions to a judge. It can offer financial benefits and move the process along quickly when money matters are not the subject of major dispute. Best of all, unlike a trial, mediation is not an adversarial proceeding. No matter how amicable both sides attempt to be, trials are about winning and losing. That experience can exacerbate existing problems and lead to at least the appearance of an imbalance of power between the separated parties, an imbalance that can lead to years of painful and draining power struggles in postdivorce interactions.

Should you choose mediation, you will still need to have your own attorney review the final agreement unless, of course, he or she participated in writing it. Each party must have his or her own representation—*under no circumstances*, even in the most agreeable of separations, should one attorney advise both parties.

Matrimonial Attorneys

Matrimonial attorneys deal primarily with the division of assets and, when contested, the custodial arrangements for the children. The more you are able to be honest with yourself and your attorney about constraints of time and finance, the better things will go in the long run. Perhaps your initial desire is to continue to pay the mortgage on the existing family home, but added living expenses will require taking an additional job. It might be time to consider options. Will the second job keep you from spending time with your children? Is maintaining the status quo worth missing weekends and holidays? Is there some way your ex could make a greater financial contribution? It is important to not let pride or a fear of further disrupting the children's lives lead you to make decisions that could decrease your opportunities to participate in their lives. Every aspect of your finances must be carefully reviewed. Marital debt, health insurance costs, alimony, child support, tax ramifications, the children's college education, pension and retirement—a matrimonial attorney will help you assess and plan for each of these issues and avoid uncertainties that could cause real problems in the future.

When it comes to custody issues, precision is also vital. Don't rely on memory or assumption for the children's vacation schedules, summer camp plans, or even annual trips to the doctor or dentist. Work out well in advance a schedule for holidays and celebrations, and then go on to decide under what circumstances (such as an unexpected opportunity to travel or the illness of a loved one) you'd be willing to alter these arrangements. Determining as precisely and fairly as possible both access to and responsibility for the children's time and lives is vital for them and you.

Therapists

In addition to an attorney and a mediator, a family therapist can play a pivotal role in aiding you with custody issues. A therapist's most important function is to act as a constant reminder of the children's needs. He or she will advise you on how to plan for their continued care—not just physical and financial but emotional as well. Needless to say, a significant effort should be made to keep the children "out of the middle." While this sounds good and reasonable, doing it can be quite difficult. Divorce is usually accompanied by anger, bitterness, and blame; generally each spouse feels that he or she has been wronged by the other.

Far too often a vicious cycle of "he said," "she said" begins, with each side accusing the other, rehashing time and again a history of "wrongs." Not only is this not constructive, it does real harm to the children who must listen to their parents tear each other apart. When parents allow their own anger to get the better of their parental judgment in this fashion, children are often sucked into a struggle for control that drains them of their ability to develop normally and robs them of much of their remaining—and precious—childhood. The sadness, anxiety, and anger children are certain to feel in a divorce under the best of circumstances can become overwhelming when parents lose control.

In the worst-case scenarios of parental conflict, rancorous parents will attempt to elicit sympathy and support from neighbors, family members, friends, school staff, medical personnel, and, of course, their own children. In such overwhelming situations children may tend to develop a chameleon-like persona, doing or saying whatever they think will please the parent or adult they're with. This desire to please can have grave consequences, affecting character development and leaving the child vulnerable to predators.

Given the opportunity, and parents willing to see the errors of their ways, a therapist can—with varying degrees of success—intervene and help turn the tide in such situations. For therapy to work, however, both parties must make a sincere, consistent, and dedicated effort to put aside their own needs in favor of the needs of their children.

Throughout the book, we present relevant real-life scenarios. These case stories are based on some of our own experiences but have been modified to protect the privacy of our clients. Some stories will illustrate how families, working together, can turn things around. Others will act as unfortunate reminders of what can happen when families won't work together. Each concludes with lessons to be learned from these families' experiences.

Daria and Steve

High School Sweethearts Who Simply Grew Apart

Daria and Steve were high school sweethearts who married shortly after graduation. During the first six years of marriage they had three children, whom they raised in the same town where they'd grown up. Marital trouble began when Daria took a part-time job and no longer kept up the housekeeping like she did when she'd been at home full-time. Sensing that Daria was not as interested in the marriage as she'd once been, Steve began following his days working construction by going out with friends at night. He also started an affair with a woman he and Daria had grown up with. When Daria learned of the relationship, she insisted Steve move out, and they eventually divorced.

After the divorce was finalized, it was revealed that Daria had a secret of her own—she, too, carried on an affair with a married colleague from work. And it was during her colleague's divorce that the truth came to light. When Steve learned she had strayed as well, he was furious. Their fragile relationship, and reasonably successful custody agreement, fell apart.

Until this revelation, Daria had been the primary caretaker, and Steve had visitation every other weekend and midweek with ample vacation visits and shared holidays. In the light of this new information, Steve came to believe the divorce settlement was a sham. He wanted to return to court and revisit all issues. He now believed that his child support payments were far too high and that Daria should have been forced to get a higher-paying or additional job in order to split the financial burdens fifty-fifty.

As their communication deteriorated, both Steve and Daria were advised to seek counseling. Fortunately, both had the presence of mind to know that therapy would be a less expensive, more expedient, and more empowering remedy than a return to court. Aware of the difficulties involved in choosing a clinician that both would be satisfied with, they agreed to accept the recommendation of their children's pediatrician.

Although the agreement to see a counselor was a good indicator for success, it was merely the beginning of a difficult process. Both parties felt the need to "win over" the clinician and present themselves in a positive light. They had lost their ability to communicate, and the children were suffering as a result. Their grades were slipping; they were irritable. The oldest, a thirteen-year-old boy, was having a difficult time, with no safe place to vent his feelings.

It took several sessions for Steve and Daria to understand that the purpose of therapy was not to rehash old issues and be declared "right," but rather to develop the ability to communicate more civilly and consistently regarding the children. The first step was establishing a safe and neutral place for their oldest son to talk about the many changes in his life, changes over which he had no control. While they wanted to blame each other, they couldn't deny their son's problems, and the pediatrician was able to recommend a treatment referral that was mutually agreed upon.

Once their son's treatment was under way, the next task was to establish a less volatile means of communication. Talking consistently ended with fighting, so a checklist was developed to help cut down on new communication tensions. Checklists of this nature are structured to keep everyone focused on the current conflict and to help each person to listen respectfully and to articulate concerns calmly and appropriately.

Over time, both Steve and Daria were able to own up to their own mistakes and were able to see that whatever had gone wrong, they had produced three wonderful children. The longer they stayed in treatment, the easier it became for them to focus on the present and their future as coparents of their children. Hostilities subsided, and though the anger never disappeared entirely, they were able to keep it from interfering with their job as parents.

What Steve and Daria were dealing with were hostilities common to many separated couples. Fortunately for them and for their children, emotional and physical abuse and neglect were not at issue. The negativity each expressed about the other in front of the children, while harmful, was a result of spontaneous anger and didn't involve planning, manipulation, or lies. Because they weren't driven by the desire to co-opt their children's affections from each other, they were encouraged by the positive effect dealing calmly with each other had on the children. This focus let them hone their communication skills to the point where they could realistically revisit their financial issues.

At this point, both attorneys agreed there was no likelihood that the court would make changes in child support or other financial arrangements. Daria, however, agreed not only to use her tax return to buy their youngest son his first bike but also to put both her and Steve's name on the card. This breakthrough move brought about Steve's real appreciation, and it was a powerful positive for all of their future dealings. Now when issues come up, they periodically revisit their therapist and work together to keep communication going smoothly.

Lessons to learn from Steve and Daria's experience:

- *Establish expectations early.* Clearly, as a young married couple, Daria and Steve were too inexperienced and immature to consider the ramifications of growth and change. Steve viewed Daria's desire to do something new in her life as a form of abandonment.
- *Secrets catch up with you.* It's no surprise that Daria didn't want to tell Steve that she, too, was unfaithful. However, when Steve found out about her deception, he understandably felt he'd taken an unfair share of the blame. His anger was not surprising or unwarranted.
- *Your negative actions quickly affect your children.* While it's all too easy to vent, keep in mind that you chose to be a parent, and although you may not have chosen to divorce, at least you have some say in the process. Your children feel powerless in this situation; don't add to their grief by making them choose between their parents.
- *Focusing on your children and their future may be the quickest route past your anger.* After all, they are proof that you and your spouse did something right. The rewards of watching your children flourish are far greater than the momentary satisfaction of raging at your ex-spouse.

Anne and Barry

A Couple Who Put Their Child's Needs Before Their Own

For eight years, Anne and Barry stayed in a marriage that was plagued by verbal abuse. They had one child, Sonja, who was six at the time they divorced. After Barry left the house, Sonja, who had always slept soundly, began refusing to go to bed and, once she did, woke intermittently throughout the night calling for her father. She became insistent that she would never be able to sleep again unless her father came home. Both Anne and Barry were focused on Sonja's emotional health, so they put aside their differences and developed a plan together. They agreed that Barry would come to the home every night and read Sonja a bedtime story. This gave Sonja more time to adjust to the fact that Barry no longer lived in the home. Eventually Sonja got used to the idea, and Barry was able to cease his nightly visits.

Lessons to learn from Anne and Barry:

- *Put the needs of your child first.* Getting past short-term issues of anger can greatly improve your child's long-term happiness and security.
- *Understand that your child's timetable is not the same as your own.* Just because you're ready to sever the ties doesn't mean your child is ready to fully cope. Try to find ways to help him ease into the new life, albeit ones that don't encourage unrealistic hopes of parental reconciliation.

Separation by Death

There is no experience equal to the death of a loved one. No matter your age, background, or experience, you cannot be prepared for that finality until you yourself go through it. A child's earliest experiences of death often involve a family pet or perhaps a grandparent or elderly neighbor. Sadly, though, others lose a parent, either through illness or an accident. How children experience and cope with that loss is influenced by several factors—their age and stage of development, whether or not death has been discussed in the home, and how fully they are allowed to participate in the family's grieving process.

Children's experiences of death vary with age. Very young children cannot understand much about death, or any type of permanence for that matter. They view the world around them primarily as an extension of themselves: as long as they exist, so does everything—and everyone—else.

During the preschool years, children become increasingly aware of the comings and goings of others and begin to understand that they are separate. Still, the permanence of death isn't something they can comprehend. It's quite common for children at this age to repeatedly ask when the deceased is coming back.

In their elementary school years, children come to the realization that death and other events in life are indeed permanent. At this time children can begin to have real difficulty experiencing loss. They feel sadness because they are able to fully understand that the person they loved will not be coming back. They may experience guilt, remembering an unkind comment they now wish they hadn't made or a chance to see the deceased that they passed up in favor of a friend's party or a ball game.

Finally, as children progress into early adolescence, they are able to view death as both permanent and a necessary part of the human experience.

Talking About Death with Children

Death is an extremely difficult issue for most people, and so many parents avoid discussing the topic until there is an urgent need to do so. Unfortunately, at that point the child's ability to process and understand what's happened is impaired by the upset and confusion he may feel. Taking a more proactive approach to discussing death may not be easy, but should the unexpected happen, it could make a big difference in a child's ability to deal with the trauma.

For many children, the first real and personal loss they experience is the death of a pet. Don't minimize or attempt to brush aside this experience and the feelings that go with it; instead, take the opportunity to let the child go through the process of grieving. Talk about what happened to the pet. Have a ritual to accompany the pet's passing—you can bury a turtle with pomp and circumstance or hold a wake for the golden retriever who won't be spending eternity in your backyard. Let the child decide what kind of ritual he would like—if he wants to throw a party or turn Rover's bone into a decorative display for his room, don't discourage him in favor of more traditional practices. Everyone deals with death differently—the point is to face it. Who knows, you might learn something from your child about coping with a difficult circumstance.

When it comes to the loss of a primary caretaker, the negative impact can affect even an infant who's grown used to the sight, smell, and touch of the same, special person every day. Transferring his care to one new person as consistently as possible is vital in such situations. Infants need as much security and consistency as possible—overwhelming them with a variety of caretakers can be at best unproductive, and at worst it can cause real problems later on.

Once a child is skilled at verbal communication, telling him about death must be done honestly and truthfully. Using such vague explanations as "Grandma is sleeping" may seem an easier choice for you and the child at that moment, but in truth it only confuses the issue. Worse, it may lead to real problems such as the child being unable to fall asleep because of unnecessary fears such as "If Grandma isn't waking up, will I?" It's not surprising that adults sometimes skirt the issue in this way—it can stem from anything from a personal fear of death to a protective urge not to share painful news or experiences with a child. Whatever the reason, it's an impulse that must be avoided. Death, along with many other difficult occurrences, is an integral part of the human experience, and it's the job of adults to prepare children for the painful as well as the pleasant—to be there for them during life's ups and downs rather than trying to protect them from the downs.

Death is a common theme in many children's books, and these can be a good place to start a simple discussion of the subject. News stories surrounding the death of a well-known person can be an easy bridge to a difficult topic. Family television shows sometimes address the topic of death and can be helpful tools, as they also deal with the reactions of children of a variety of ages. Whatever medium suits you best, using a book, news event, or television show to broach this difficult topic could make a big difference when you need help the most.

When you talk to a child about death, do it in plain language he can easily understand. Be willing to take as much time as necessary to sit and talk with him and answer any questions he might have. Young children, in particular, may ask the same question over and over again. Simply be patient and answer the question. Many times, particularly when a child has had no experience with death, he will not even know what questions to ask. Be prepared to offer an explanation of what has happened to the person who has died. Of course, if you have a specific religious belief, this will be of great help during the conversation. If your vision of the afterlife is not so clearly defined, try to focus on the fact that although a person's body is no longer present, he or she remains in our memories and our affections. Avoid frightening imagery or too much information; a detailed description of cremation or embalming is more than most children can or should have to cope with.

Allow Children to Be Part of the Grieving Process

The rituals associated with death—attending a funeral, wake, or memorial service—are a concrete way of beginning to accept a death along with acknowledging the gifts of the departed loved one's life. As with all issues of development, the ability to deal with such an event varies from child to child. Allow your child to participate at the level he feels comfortable. A wake celebrating Grandpa might be a happy, comforting event for a child who can see the love that person inspired among family and friends. However, viewing Grandpa in an open casket might be too frightening and confusing for the same child. Listen to the child closely, and you'll know what he feels safe doing, what frightens him, and what he might be doing simply to please you. Again, remember for both you and him that there is no "right way" to grieve. Some young children want to fully participate in the process and benefit from this; others need more time to cope with the death and are best served by not participating. Whatever happens, don't force a child to do something that clearly upsets him. The scars could last a lifetime.

A child needs to feel he has as much of a right to be a part of the grieving process as any other member of the family. Allowing him to participate as much as he wants to can be of benefit not only for him but for the whole family. It is also important to acknowledge—for both you and him—that when it comes to the loss of someone important, the sadness may never entirely go away. Assure him that there is no preordained time for grieving to end and that it varies from individual to individual.

Lessons to learn:

- Take a proactive approach to dealing with the process of death. Don't wait for a tragedy to address this difficult topic.
- Understand that the ability to deal with death is directly related to a child's age and developmental level.
- Listen patiently to a child's questions about death, and answer them as honestly and simply as possible.
- Allow the child to participate in the grieving possible as much as he wants to. Never push a child to be involved if it makes him uncomfortable or upset.

2

Dynamics of the Basic Stepfamily

ACCORDING TO THE U.S. Census Bureau, more than half of all first marriages eventually end in divorce, with about 75 percent of divorced persons remarrying and about 63 percent of remarriages involving children from a prior marriage. Sixty percent of remarriages eventually end in divorce.

Roughly thirty-five million stepfamilies exist in the United States today. More than thirteen hundred stepfamilies are forming daily, with one out of three Americans being part of a stepfamily. In addition to the usual elements of attraction and commitment, adults rebounding from a difficult separation may often look to the new relationship to provide healing or, at the least, soothe the wounds caused by death or divorce. They imagine one big, new, happy family that will make up for the unhappiness, hurts, and disappointments of past events.

Meanwhile, the children involved are entertaining fantasies of their own, primarily the reunification wish that their parents will get back together and life will be ideal once again. This fantasy may occur even after a difficult divorce during which a child may have actually expressed the belief that his or her parents would be better apart. Certainly when abuse is involved, a child may be relieved when divorce occurs, but there are others who long for the family to be back together even after experiencing physical, sexual, or emotional abuse. Children have an enormous ability to forgive, so when their parents separate simply because of incompatibility, they often hold out hope that things may return to normal and that the family will reconnect.

Aside from the hope that their parents will reconcile, children can also become accustomed to being the primary focus of attention when they're with one of their separated parents. A new routine forms, new rituals are shared, and children naturally become very protective of this newly negotiated relationship. At some point after this new routine is established, the parent may feel secure and confident, ready to enter a new and potentially serious relationship. The children, on the other hand, are also feeling newly happy and secure, and they are likely uninterested in a new person who will bring disruption to their lives. Adults in the process of blending their families clearly need to take these factors into account. Newly formed families must develop methods of allowing relationships to grow accordingly instead of forcing a situation in a way that could create real problems down the line.

Unfortunately, there are no magic words that can convince children that the parent's love for someone new in no way means he or she loves the children less. Nor is there any standardized phrase the new adult can utter that will convince the children that he or she has no intention of trying to steal affection away from the children or impose him- or herself as a new parent. Bringing a new group together is a work in progress, a process that must be undertaken slowly and with the certain knowledge that there will be plenty of challenges and misunderstandings along the way.

The person assuming the new parental role is clearly the outsider. If two people with children marry, they will encounter the double complication of each parent being viewed as an outsider by the separate and distinct sets of children. While this may be an unpleasant prospect, the truth is that, for awhile at least, the "outsider" parent becomes an ideal target for the children's negative feelings and actions and the perfect person to blame for their upsets and negative experiences.

David and Allison

The Wicked Stepmother Complex

David was the divorced father of four girls. Although his ex-wife, Kathryn, was the girls' primary caretaker, David had a regular and positive visitation schedule of every other weekend. He also had a longtime girlfriend, Allison, herself the mother of two, with whom his daughters were quite comfortable. All that changed, however, when David and Allison moved in together with Allison's daughters. From that moment on, David's daughters viewed Allison as evil incarnate, even though she had done nothing but try to be their friend.

In addition to alienating themselves from Allison, David's daughters made serious and sometimes successful attempts to turn their mother, Kathryn, against Allison by twisting and distorting information about her. Because Kathryn had some residual feelings of anger toward David, it wasn't hard to convince her that Allison was mistreating her daughters. As a result of their manipulations, the girls began to acquire a great deal of power within both their mother's and father's houses. Kathryn became convinced that she needed to rescue her girls from a bad situation, and that, combined with her longtime guilt over the divorce, led her to let the girls get away with far more than they had previously. Second chances rather than immediate consequences became the order of the day. Although the girls might have momentarily enjoyed pushing the limits, ultimately it brought them no real happiness. Being able to get away with bad behavior destabilized their lives. They lost their former sense of predictability and, with it, their sense of emotional safety. As a result, their acting out escalated until professional treatment became a necessity.

During therapy sessions, several things became clear. The girls wanted to maintain a certain degree of ownership over their father. They deeply resented the fact that they no longer saw David on a daily basis, but Allison's daughters did. Finally, they were angry over the fact that Allison's daughters were present during their weekend visits and they had to share him during their abbreviated time together.

Treatment addressed both emotional and practical issues. On the emotional end, therapy helped them accept the fact that their father's feelings for them hadn't changed. Therapy gave them a safe arena in which to talk to the adults in their lives so that they could fully communicate their feelings and develop a higher level of trust. On a practical level, the living arrangements during the girls' visitation were addressed. David had purposely arranged to have his girls' visits coincide with the weekends Allison's girls were with them so that they could get to know each other and enjoy activities together because all the girls were close in age.

Unfortunately, these good intentions went sour, as the last thing David's girls wanted was a distraction from time with their father. Once Allison's girls started spending those weekends with their own father, the connection between David and his daughters improved, and eventually so did their relationship with Allison.

Lessons to be learned from David and Allison's situation:

- *Understand that cohabitation is a huge issue.* In David's daughters' minds, moving in meant that Allison went from a person who was in their father's life to someone who was replacing them in their father's life.
- *Be in charge.* Chaos ensued when David and his ex-wife, Kathryn, gave in to their children because of guilt and anger. Indulging a child may feel good in the

short term, and it may bring about the momentary reward of being the favored parent, but in the long term, a lack of rules and order is simply destructive.

- *Don't try to force relationships.* David wanted the girls to get along, but he didn't factor in that they'd need time and room to do it on their own. Don't assume you know what would make your children comfortable and happy—talk to them about it.
- *When things get out of hand, a neutral party is called for.* In this scenario, the girls had done a fine job of manipulating both facts and emotions. A therapist was able to sort things out by providing a forum that was not about taking sides but improving the situation. Once misconceptions were cleared up, the parents were able to gain control of the situation. Only then did parent-child relations improve considerably.

Larry and Kendra

A Cautious Couple Sets the Tone for Avoiding Confrontation

When Larry and Kendra met, both were divorced and each had one young son. Larry's divorce had been extremely difficult, one filled with anger and extensive litigation over petty issues. As a result, he was highly concerned about the potential for any further trouble with his ex-wife and proceeded with a great deal of thoughtfulness and caution. Conversely, Kendra's divorce was mutually desirable and civilized, so she was able to enter into the blending process with a positive and open mind-set.

For very different reasons, both Kendra and Larry were committed to clear and consistent communication with their former spouses regarding their upcoming marriage. Both parties also involved their six- and seven-year-old sons in the wedding plans. They presented this new marriage as an opportunity for the boys to have another loving grown-up in their lives, and they emphasized that each new parent would in no way replace their own mother or father. They explained the difference between the new stepparent and the biological parent to reassure the boys and to lessen any threat that their former spouses might feel. This further smoothed the way to successfully implementing the blending process. Although the family had not scheduled a course of therapy, Larry and Kendra did periodically consult a family counselor, who helped them explore a variety of possible choices in difficult scenarios and validate the decisions they made.

An unexpected positive result came out of Larry and Kendra's cautious approach. Shortly after their marriage, Larry's ex-wife announced that she was in a new relationship. She was able to put her anger behind her and apply Larry and Kendra's respectful treatment of the blending process into her own new relationship and family.

Lessons to be learned from Larry and Kendra:

- *Get over it*. If you want to have a solid future, you need to put the past behind you. Somebody has to begin the process of being positive. By concerning himself with avoiding further confrontation and not dwelling on the past, Larry was able to make the best of what could have been a very bad situation.
- *Respect your ex*. By working to make sure that both the children and their parents understand that neither new spouse is taking over the role of Mom or Dad,

potentially unpleasant scenarios of competition and
anger are avoided.
- *Set an example.* By getting on with your life, you can
open the door for your ex to get on with his or hers. A
respectful and positive attitude can be as contagious
as a negative and disparaging one.

Once the initial blending process is achieved, the long-term business of successfully living together can begin.

Creating a Blueprint for the Blended Household

After the initial "getting acquainted" period, a newly formed family
enters a restructuring process. This involves establishing rules, schedules, and communication styles for the new family unit. For a child living between two households, this likely means that she will be dealing
regularly with two different sets of rules and expectations. Even when
the biological parents agree on basics such as curfew, dating age,
acceptable grade point averages, and so on, differences in parenting
styles inevitably emerge. For instance, it may be perfectly acceptable
to leave your bicycle in the middle of Dad's living room, but doing so
at Mom's house would cause some real friction. Add new spouses to
this equation, and the importance of clearly and thoughtfully discussing and establishing basic house rules becomes clear.

Creating a blueprint for a successfully blended family involves an
often-lengthy process of negotiation. The first stage should be between
the new partners who clearly need to establish what they will and won't
put up with in their own home. Second, they should be sure that nothing they decide is directly and harmfully at odds with rules established
by the former spouses. For instance, if one parent is seriously opposed
to a child riding in a car with a newly licensed teenage driver, the other

parent should respect that concern rather than permit such behavior during the time the child is with him or her. When it comes to less vital concerns, like whether a child can wear jeans to school or must be in bed by 11 P.M. as opposed to 10 P.M., these should be decided by each household and mutually respected by the separate ex-spouses.

Once the parents have determined what issues are not negotiable, it's time to involve the children and create a solid basis for communication within the new family unit. Likely topics for negotiation include homework schedules, use of the television and computer, and the division and assignment of chores. Give everyone a chance to be heard. Create a family contract that allows everyone a reference point for rules and behavior. This contract cannot, of course, be ironclad. Trial and error will likely reveal necessary revisions, and, as children grow up, adjustments must be made accordingly. However, at the very least the contract allows you to maintain a solid basis from which to begin a discussion. Moving forward without clear communication can be disastrous.

Hobart and Beth

Stepchildren Engaged in Turf Wars

Hobart and Beth's marriage was the second for both of them. Each had two daughters from a previous marriage, and the girls were about the same age. Hobart and Beth were very excited about the prospects for a successful union and were certain that the girls would bond.

Both families had the same custodial agreement—the mothers were the primary caretakers, and the fathers had extensive weekend and vacation visitation. Hobart moved in with Beth and her girls, who lived in the original family home she shared with her former spouse and received after the divorce proceedings. Hobart's daughters came regularly to visit. Beth and Hobart spent this initial time focusing on what they thought was the positive—the likelihood that their daughters would share the same interests, be involved in the same types of studies in school, and so on. Unfortunately, while trying to look on the upside, they ignored the very real problems and tensions that were growing within the house.

The heart of the problems between the new stepsisters was the very primal issue of turf. At home, Hobart's daughters had their own rooms; at Beth's they were required to share with her daughters. None of the girls liked this arrangement. Beth's girls felt intruded on; Hobart's felt unwelcome. The results were numerous accusations and counteraccusations of stealing and defacing property and complaints about how each set of daughters was being put upon by the other. With no established basis for communication and each group feeling angry and unheard, the situation escalated. The girls became extremely territorial about friends and extended family members, and what had once seemed to be a potentially happy stepsibling relationship became bitterly adversarial. Still, the parents failed to acknowledge and address this escalating situation until finally Beth's eldest daughter engaged in a fistfight with Hobart's youngest daughter, resulting in a broken finger that landed one of the girls in an emergency room. The hospital social worker was called in to speak to the family and, after some conversation, recommended counseling. Finally, Hobart and Beth were able to acknowledge the gravity of the situation and agreed that some relief was necessary.

The first step involved sessions with a therapist who was experienced in negotiations between siblings. Working with different combinations of family members, she put together an initial agreement that kept everybody safe, if not happy. Next, the therapist sent the girls to a counselor of their own and continued her work with Hobart and Beth, eventually involving their former spouses as well. The willingness of all four biological parents to work together was a real benefit because it improved adult communication and created a far more consistent message for the girls.

One result of these sessions was that Beth's daughters were invited to spend time with Hobart's girls at their home. Beth's girls had a chance to know how it felt to be the "outsider," and Hobart's girls got a clear picture of what it meant to have their private space encroached upon. As a result, they started to really talk to each other, not only about issues of territory and privacy, but about how it felt to have their biological parent spend more time with their stepsiblings. In fact, once rules and boundaries were established to the extent that the therapist and the parents were able to step back, the girls did the bulk of healing and relationship building on their own.

Lessons to learn from Hobart and Beth's story:

- *Be wary of your own expectations.* Hobart and Beth began their life together with extraordinarily unrealistic visions of how it would go. Reality is difficult enough without first having to overcome a carefully crafted fantasy.
- *Ignoring problems won't make them go away.* Beth and Hobart were attached to the way they hoped things would be, which clouded their ability to see the reality of the way things really were.
- *Children have many of the same needs as adults.* If Beth and Hobart had taken the time to imagine what it would mean to suddenly be forced to share a living space with other adults they barely knew, they might have considered how the same situation would affect their children and started a dialogue much sooner than they did.
- *Get professional help.* In the case of Hobart and Beth, a physical injury caused a social worker's involvement. It shouldn't take a trip to the ER to know things have gotten out of hand.

- *Get your ex-spouse involved whenever possible.* Although some former spouses will use trouble in the new household only as a way to drive a wedge between the children and the other parent, this is generally not true. Most parents are interested in the best possible life for their children and can put aside their differences in order to work together toward that end.
- *Give kids the room to work it out.* Once stability and boundaries have been achieved, children have a remarkable ability to communicate with each other. At some point, when they can safely do so, adults need to step out of the way and let children create a real, rather than an imposed, peace.

Bart and Suzanne

Taking a Proactive Approach to Blending Households

With time and planning, it is possible for things to go well from the beginning. The story of Bart and Suzanne may not at first glance seem to apply to most people because they had luxuries of time and financial resources that most people don't have. However, as anyone who reads the gossip columns knows, money is in no way an indicator of an amicable or easy family life. Many of Bart and Suzanne's choices could be applied to anyone's situation, albeit on a more modest scale.

When Bart and Suzanne met, she was a divorcée with two children—a boy, eight, and a girl, ten; he was a widower with two teenagers—a son, sixteen, and a daughter, seventeen. Suzanne had received the suburban, middle-class family home in the divorce settlement. She and the children were very connected to their community, involved in church and school activities, and surrounded by extended maternal family with a lot of contact with cousins. Bart and his children lived in a three-bedroom co-op in a major city with a doorman and regular access to museums, theater, and a busy urban life.

When Suzanne and Bart decided to marry, her children were fond of him, but she didn't know his children well. On the plus side, because of their age differences, the contact between future stepsiblings had been pleasant, without the typical control issues that occur when children are closer in age.

It was decided that after the wedding Suzanne and the children would move into Bart's home in the city so that he could remain near his office. Additionally, both parents felt it would be easier for Suzanne's children to adjust to the move than it would be for the teenagers, who were in their final high school years. Still, they recognized that there would be real issues for Suzanne's children, who would be both separated from familiar surroundings and family and thrust into an urban environment.

Suzanne and Bart were determined to have the transition go as well as possible, so they sought a therapist for some objective, professional advice on how to handle the move. Fortunately, both had families who were supportive of their new relationship, particularly Bart's children, who were looking forward to college and the next stage of their lives and who were delighted that their father had found someone. Bart's children genuinely liked Suzanne and her children, so the pluses of their new siblings outweighed the minuses.

Wisely, Bart and Suzanne paid careful attention to the issue of living space. As the co-op had only three bedrooms, two of the children would need to double up. It was decided to make a very small study into a room for Suzanne's daughter. Bart's daughter would keep her own room that had long been her refuge in a male-dominated house. The two boys, who used their bedrooms primarily to sleep and store dirty clothes, would share Bart's son's room. To make the room more spacious, built-in bookshelves and storage units were added and replaced freestanding furniture. All of the children were given a voice in this transition, but Bart and Suzanne maintained the final say. Once the decisions of "what to do" had been made, "how to do it" was next on the list.

Again taking the advice of the counselor, as the wedding grew near, Suzanne and the children spent increasing amounts of time in the co-op and participated more and more in city life. Her children began to find advantages in their new home. Her son was thrilled to be able to attend major league baseball games; her daughter made a friend in the co-op and began attending dance classes with her. The child-friendly doorman played his part by producing the occasional piece of unexpected candy.

Over time Suzanne's children began bringing pictures and toys from home to the co-op. Suzanne's daughter, who'd learned to love gardening from her grandmother, made a window box of plants from her garden and placed them on the balcony of the seventeenth-floor residence. Visits from Suzanne's family, voicing encouragement and excitement, further helped the process. This gradual transition had a remarkable reward—even before they completed the final move, Suzanne's children referred to the co-op as "our house."

As a final move toward familial togetherness, Suzanne purchased a small vacation home near the ocean with the money from the sale of her suburban home. It provided a place the newly blended family could truly call theirs, with the additional benefit of a tiny yard and garden to replace the one Suzanne's children had left behind.

Even if you can't afford a big-city co-op or a cottage by the sea, there are many positives to be learned from Bart and Suzanne's scenario:

- *Be proactive.* By realistically anticipating difficulties and talking to a professional about potential pitfalls and how to avoid them, Bart and Suzanne avoided creating tensions among their children that might have resulted from rushing the process.

- *Respect your children's right to space and privacy.* Rather than thrusting the children together as they saw fit, Bart and Suzanne negotiated the best—if imperfect—deal for everyone. In the case of Suzanne's young daughter, converting the small study gave her the privacy she needed. When it comes to a place of their own, for many children size is not an issue.

- *Take your time. Blending is a gradual process.* Even if you can't afford the luxury of maintaining two residences for an extended period, find ways to ease into the situation. Maybe that means creating two tiny bedrooms from one small one or arranging a weeklong campout in the backyard where kids can spend time in a neutral space. It may mean that a child brings her wardrobe in piece by piece rather than in one wrenching move.

- *When the time is right, make changes in the residence that reflect the presence of a new family unit.* Choose and assemble an entertainment unit, work together to plant a garden, repaint the living room—anything you can do that makes the home a reflection of the new family unit.

As one considers the step toward blending already existing family units, there are often questions about when to involve the children. The most important answer is, not before you are sure as adults of your commitment to each other. What children don't need are more experiences of failed relationships, which will further leave them feeling abandoned or rejected in some way.

Divided Loyalties

Bear in mind that when there are difficulties between adults, children struggle with loyalty issues. Clearly with divorce there is the initial trauma of divided loyalties between the biological parents. When one parent moves on to a new relationship, these loyalty issues are exacerbated. One problem may lie with the biological parent who has been "left behind." He or she may often, and within earshot of the child, express negative feelings about the ex-spouse's new partner. This leaves the child feeling that if she likes one parent's new partner, she'll be letting the other parent down and that that parent will no longer want to be involved with her. These situations are often worsened when one parent is able to move on with life more easily than the other. The natural reaction of the child is to feel sorry for the parent who is alone and resentful of the parent with a new relationship. Unfortunately, there is often a tendency on the part of the unconnected parent to reinforce the "poor me" idea, which only intensifies stress on the children.

Frequently the child of a first marriage has problems integrating into the family of the second. This is especially true if there are preexisting emotional or behavioral problems. In many instances the child feels rejected and is quite vocal about letting others know how she feels. The newly attached parent is often consumed with guilt as a result. The child may manipulate the new relationship, using the "I was here first" tactic to vie for parental attention, sometimes in the hope that she can effect her parents' reunification.

Andrew

Establishing Stepparent Roles

Andrew was six years old with parents who had divorced as a result of the father's substance abuse. His parents' marriage was brief, and after the divorce Andrew had little contact with his father. When the boy was two, his mother remarried a man who was very attentive to Andrew. Eventually Andrew's biological father cleaned up his act and started to become reinvolved in his son's life. At the same time, his father married a woman who had two young children from a previous marriage. This sudden reemergence of his father, along with his father's new family, created significant ambivalence in Andrew regarding the emotional safety and consistency of his connection to his father.

Unfortunately, Andrew developed various emotional difficulties that had significant impact on his behavior. This created enormous stress for his mother and stepfather whose relationship became strained. It seemed that some of Andrew's problems (impulsive and hyperactive behaviors) had a biological basis, as his father had a history of similar difficulties.

Both of the biological parents were able to agree upon the facts: Andrew was hard to manage, and his behavioral deficits were evident while he spent time with each parent. Despite the agreement, there was discord. Andrew's stepmother did not understand why the father needed separate time alone with Andrew during family visits, and she made it very clear that she was unhappy with Andrew calling her "Mom." The truth is, while this may be unnerving to adults, it is a regular and not particularly significant behavior for young children to address an adult figure in such a manner. Usually it is an issue only for the grown-up.

The process of family treatment focused on helping the stepparents to better understand the importance of their roles. They were made to see the direct correlation between Andrew's behavior and the depth of their connection to him. Strategies for better management of Andrew's and their own behaviors and emotional states were developed. Andrew's stepfather was able to understand his own initial feelings of rejection after the biological father returned to the family picture and how, in turn, his change in attitude toward Andrew caused the boy to feel rejection. In the case of Andrew's biological mother, she came to understand her husband's conflicts and worked with him to develop a style comparable to her own for managing Andrew. This process helped Andrew to feel less rejected.

Additionally, Andrew felt unhappy about needing to share his newly formed connection with his father with two new stepsiblings. Andrew's biological father was receptive to understanding that Andrew felt displaced by the new children in his father's life. He took a new approach that altered their weekend visits to regularly include special time alone together, in addition to mutually appealing activities involving all three children. Thus, Andrew began to develop a greater sense of security in his relationships with all family members.

Lessons to be learned from Andrew's situation:

- *Communicate.* All of the adults involved need to communicate with one another and respect the fact that children may not "blend" as readily as the adults would like.
- *Value the role of each biological parent.* The importance of the role each biological parent, even if absent, plays in the lives of his or her children must not be minimized.
- *Recognize the importance of the biological parent-child relationship.* The special qualities of this relationship should be celebrated. Placing importance on this relationship, though, does not have to devalue any relationship between stepparents and stepchildren.
- *Encourage positive relationships.* It is possible, indeed preferable, for children to enjoy positive relationships with all of the parent figures in their lives.

Adolescents and the Blended Family

When addressing the issues of children in blended family situations, special attention should be paid to the plight of the adolescent. Adolescents do not respond well to disruption in their lives. This is a time of extraordinary change and a marked tendency to become extremely self-focused. While the emerging adolescent is striving for individuality by separating and rebelling against parental constraints and guidelines, they nonetheless want their island of security (i.e., Mom and Dad) to remain stable. In effect, they need a constant to rebel against. Additionally, adolescents want control, and a parental breakup represents something that they have no control over. The result is anger and/or depression. Frequently, adolescents will take sides in a divorce and blame what is happening on one or both parents or, sometimes, on themselves. Adolescents also struggle with practical issues such as "Will we have to move?" "How will we get by?" "Why are you doing this?" and "What did you do to make Mom/Dad leave?" The parent who remains with the child may face verbal bashing from the adolescent, but he or she could also find him- or herself the subject of sympathy, with the adolescent's anger directed toward the departing spouse. Whatever his or her role, it behooves the parent to take an objective stance and not encourage one behavior or the other but rather help the adolescent see that blame need not be assigned, nor is it necessary to choose one parent over the other.

When it comes to dealing with issues of loyalty and competition, it's important to put yourself in the child's place and imagine how she is struggling with such daily issues as whom to listen to and what and who should take priority in her life. New partners in these situations need to do some careful strategizing in terms of their roles with the child and the boundaries of discipline. One way to deal with this is to simply sit down with the child and discuss the issues of blending a family. Outline clearly the lines of authority, and demonstrate to the child that both sets of parents are a team and that all have an individual and important role in making the family work.

Keep in mind also that with adolescence comes a depth to relationships that has not existed previously. This is particularly true in relationships with the opposite gender. When a child's role models for such relationships have separated from each other, it can raise a number of confusing issues: "If people stop loving one another, is the relationship ended?" "Aren't people supposed to work out conflicts?" "Does anger and fighting always lead to dissolution?" When overwhelmed by these questions, a teen frequently retreats, sometimes to her room, sometimes to a friend's house. What brings comfort may also bring discontent. A teen may wonder why friends' parents are able to stay together while her own parents can't. Parents must take a break from their own dramas to acknowledge and deal with what is happening to their vulnerable teen. Find her a safe means—either a reassuring place to go or another person to talk to—to express her feelings. Understand that "acting out" is usually as much a cry for help as hiding out is.

Sometimes adolescents will behave badly as a way to put themselves in the forefront of activity. For these children, any attention is good attention. An objective point of view can be vital in such instances. Don't keep these behaviors hidden out of concern that you as a parent will be judged. This is a time to turn to people who aren't a part of your family for help in stabilizing the situation and providing support to these most vulnerable children.

Often when new stepparents arrive on the scene, particularly those who have not yet had children of their own, they idealize what can be achieved within the family unit. One can hardly imagine a greater clash than one that occurs between such a well-meaning but somewhat misguided parent and an adolescent child who, by virtue of her age, is testing the limits of rebellion, individuality, and challenging authority. In addition, a child of divorce has issues of loyalty both to her biological parents and to their old way of life.

Ally and Carol

"A Bull in a China Shop"

When Harry married Carol, she was his third wife. Harry's teenage daughter, Ally, lived with him as a result of ongoing problems with her less-than-functional mother. Carol, who had no children of her own, entered the situation with the certainty of a novice. Hoping to create an ideal family unit, Carol determined that she and Harry should engage in clear and consistent limit setting. Harry's parenting style was as laid-back as Carol's was take-charge. Needless to say, stress quickly began to build up in this new marriage.

Ally, unhappy with Carol's "I know what this child needs" attitude, began to exhibit behavioral difficulties. Eventually, she was brought to a therapist. The counselor offered Ally assistance in two ways. First, she served as her support and ally during this difficult adjustment period. The therapist listened to Ally talk about her typical adolescent struggles as well as her struggle to adjust to her father's remarriage. Ally had trouble accepting that this newcomer would not simply be her father's wife but insisted on acting as her parent as well.

Meanwhile the therapist helped the new couple take a realistic look at their situation. They examined the new family system that had been put into place and how it affected the adolescent girl who was experiencing conflict even before becoming an integral part of a new family unit. The newly married wife and mother learned some valuable information about adolescent issues and development. She also came to understand that there are many approaches to problem solving and that, in this particular instance, "take-charge" was not the best option. In time, a trusting and realistic relationship developed between Carol and Ally. The two established good listening skills, which became an integral part of the family's communication style.

Lessons to be learned from Ally and Carol:

- *Go slowly*. When you're new to a situation, a period of observation and understanding is vital. If it's hard to conceive of this in terms of family, imagine the workplace. We've all met the new coworker who comes in like a bull in a china shop, ready to change the status quo while assuming an inappropriate familiarity with his or her coworkers. What was your response to such a person? Discomfort, resentment, and a desire to undermine and ostracize this person would all be likely reactions. Now transfer this reality to the home. It quickly becomes apparent how anyone, let alone an adolescent being presented with an instant parent, could be upset by such behavior. This doesn't mean you should be a pushover or even allow the child to treat you with disrespect and compromise boundaries you have always set for yourself. It does mean that you can't walk into a place and simply impose yourself. There was life there before you, and, if you persist, there will be life there after you've gone.

- *Work with your spouse.* Parents, whether step or biological, must present a thoughtful united front if they are to successfully maintain the family unit. If they don't, the child will have an ideal route to divide and conquer, and the parents' relationship with each other, along with that of parent/child, will almost inevitably suffer as a result.

George

A Father Finally Finds the Right Partner

George had been married three times. He had three children from his third marriage, two of whom, Jeff age twelve and Mark age nine, lived with him. His six-year-old daughter, Susan, lived with her mother in another part of the country.

George put his boys in therapy because the breakup of his marriage was sudden and unexpected. George's wife had left the family to reestablish a relationship with her high school sweetheart some distance away.

Although the boys initially lived with their mother, after a year, she decided to move the boys back with their father while keeping her daughter with her. Needless to say, this caused the boys to feel rejected and abandoned. Although George may not have always shown the best of judgment in his relationships with women, he quickly realized that his boys needed help. Both were quite open, intelligent, and able to address their anger and confusion about their parents' split.

During the therapeutic process, George found a new mate, Martha, who happened to have two children of her own. George's boys developed a real affection toward her. Although the boys still struggled with their apparent abandonment by their mother and separation from their sister, they were able to feel safe in the love and support of their father. Additionally, Martha, who was very different from their mother, brought a new set of strengths and support that they were happy to accept.

Lessons to be learned from George's situation:

- *Be proactive.* George didn't wait for the boys to get in trouble; he saw clearly that they would be affected by their mother's actions and moved quickly to find a professional to help them cope.
- *You can't control your ex, only yourself.* George could have worsened the situation by belittling his ex or trying to get her to behave in a more appropriate and supportive manner toward her sons. Instead he focused his energies on the children, where they could do real good.

- *Even in the most difficult situations, children will flourish given real love and support.* Children have a natural instinct for survival. Give them a safe and loving environment and, with time, patience, and understanding they can overcome almost anything.

Although it is the ultimate role and responsibility of the parent to take charge, this in no way precludes taking an occasional look at the world through your child's eyes. Offering her that understanding and respect will give you an extraordinarily rich lifetime of family memories and rewards.

In this chapter we've dealt primarily with issues that can affect any stepfamily. In the next chapter, we'll address specific issues resulting from differences in racial, religious, and cultural backgrounds.

3

Blending Families with Racial, Cultural, or Religious Differences

BLENDING FAMILIES WITH racial, cultural, and/or religious differences has the added difficulties of the disapproval of family and friends, a lack of general acceptance by society, and—between the two partners—some basic and profound differences in life experiences that need to be honestly addressed if they are to be overcome.

The Interracial Blended Family

There is an increasing number of interracial marriages in the United States today. The U.S. Census Bureau predicts that the current trend toward ethnic intermarriage will continue and that by the middle of the twenty-first century 50 percent of the U.S. population will be of mixed racial descent.

Although interracial marriage may still turn heads in some parts of the country, one need only stand outside of a Los Angeles high school as the children leave for the day to see the future. Every race and creed is represented separately, as well as in combination, with the children seemingly unaware of the stir that their appearance would have made just a decade or two ago.

Ethnic blending has always been a part of the United States. We are, indeed, the world's "melting pot." Within that melting pot there are perhaps no stereotypes harder to manage than those about race. Unfortunately, racism—in forms from subtle to blatant—is still a part of American life. This can result in a number of problems for any couple attempting to create a racially blended family. Fortunately, these problems can be overcome.

Gene and Sandra

"We'll Make It Work in Spite of Them"

Gene and Sandra were both divorced when they met in the workplace. Gene was forty-three, an African-American sales manager with a thirteen-year-old daughter. Gene was not his daughter's primary custodian, but the two spent a great deal of time together and enjoyed a close relationship. The divorce between Gene and his former wife was relatively amicable, and she had since remarried a Nigerian national. Sandra, the office manager, was thirty-three when her involvement with Gene began. A Midwesterner of Scandinavian descent, Sandra had two sons, ages five and seven. The children were the product of an abusive first marriage, and their father had no involvement whatsoever in their lives.

When Gene and Sandra were dating, they encountered little opposition. Gene's former wife was acquainted with Sandra through the workplace. She was supportive of the relationship, as her daughter was fond of Sandra, and Sandra never made any attempt to undermine the mother's role.

However, once Sandra and Gene decided to marry, parents on both sides objected. Gene's parents, who had worked two and three jobs to put him through college, were horrified; they were certain that he was "throwing his life away." Although they claimed to have nothing against Sandra personally, they felt the couple was opening themselves up to more problems than anyone could reasonably manage. They pointed out to Gene the problems experienced by interracial couples that they knew and reminded him that resistance to interracial relationships was as common in the black community as it was in the white community. Gene's father expressed particular concern for his granddaughter, who would likely end up with interracial siblings who "wouldn't know where they belonged."

Sandra's family had a much more cut-and-dried response: she would have to choose. She could either marry a black man or continue to maintain a relationship with them, but she could not do both.

As a result of these conflicts, Gene and Sandra sought counseling, primarily due to concerns about the negative impact of their family's reactions on their children. They began to be concerned that they were being selfish in pursuing their relationship and wondered if their parents' reactions would be typical of what they'd encounter throughout their lives together. In the early stages of counseling, they affirmed that they were truly devoted to each other and well suited to go through life together. They took the firm stance that their relationship was a priority and that although there would certainly be difficulties, ultimately their love and devotion could only be good for their children.

During this process, Sandra's brother Roy, who had taken a less hard line than his parents and spent some actual time with Sandra and Gene, had a more positive view of the relationship. As a result, he decided to let the family know his view of the situation: "Sandra is a lot better off with Gene than she was with the white man who beat her." While less than a ringing endorsement, it seemed to make a difference, and gradually she and Gene became reconnected to family members. All members of both of their immediate families attended the wedding and bonded over their common concern that "life will be too hard for them."

Gene and Sandra's success resulted from jointly and methodically facing the world and its prejudices by insisting they be dealt with first and foremost as individuals. A racially similar couple would not have encountered the hostilities they faced, but Gene and Sandra did not allow this to tear them apart. Rather, they faced this opposition together, and that process became the basis for a meaningful support system that enabled the couple to eventually have children of their own. For Gene and Sandra, their relationship was strictly about their love for and commitment to each other; they didn't join any interracial support groups or become politically active in encouraging society as a whole to accept their decision. They simply wanted the opportunity to be together and make their own way, and so they have.

Lessons to be learned from Gene and Sandra:

- *Be willing to examine your relationship.* Rather than simply dismissing their family's concerns and bonding together in what could have been an ultimately destructive "you and me against the world" stance, Gene and Sandra asked themselves some hard questions. As a result of their confidence in their relationship being put to the test, they were able to have real certainty about the strength of their relationship that proved invaluable in the long run.

- *Offer perspective.* Once Sandra's family had to face the fact that being white didn't make her first husband a good one, they began to consider the possibility that a husband who was black might not be bad. Accepting the truth of Sandra's life—that the beatings she encountered from an abusive white husband were far more destructive than any prejudice she'd encounter with a kind, loving, and supportive black one— allowed them to take a second look and reconsider the harshness of their original position.

- *Understand generational differences.* Both Gene and Sandra's parents were from an era in which interracial marriage was not only more difficult than it is today, it was often genuinely dangerous. Ultimately, this common generational bond brought the parents together as they expressed similar concerns for their children. Recognizing those differences and similarities that transcend race can help compartmentalize and deal with family conflicts inherent in interracial relationships.
- *Do what works for you.* For some couples, sharing the problems and joys of their relationship, whether or not it's interracial, is profoundly useful. For others, family is a more individual undertaking. There is no "right" way to find your way in a sometimes hostile world, but a shared approach—and commitment to that approach no matter what input you may get from others—forms the basis of a solid and successful relationship.

Conflicts of Race and Culture

Sometimes interracial couples clash as a result of their inherent cultural differences rather than societal pressures stemming from the different colors of their skin. Behavioral predispositions don't always operate on a consistent, or even conscious, level; yet our inherited cultural identities are shaped at a very early age. Historically, racial and religious issues have presented significant blending problems—even more so than cultural issues, as previous immigrants tended to share a basic European cultural tradition. Such is no longer the case, as immigrants today represent more diverse cultural traditions. Therefore, it is more important to relinquish older stereotypic assumptions and consider culture as a potential source of conflict—perhaps even more so than race or religion. Such was the case with the marriage of Raimundo and Carla.

Raimundo and Carla

Vast Cultural Differences Divide a Marriage

Raimundo, a Hispanic man, and Carla, an Anglo woman, married for the first time for each of them after a brief courtship. Because neither had the baggage of a previous marriage or the expressed desire to have children, the couple assumed their relationship would pose no significant difficulties for either themselves or their families.

Although neither family raised any serious objections, things did not go well for Raimundo and Carla from the outset. Their problems cut across racial and cultural lines: poor communication, poorly considered common goals, and poor compatibility. However, the overriding source of marital conflict stemmed from cultural differences. Raimundo, raised on his mother's excellent home cooking, felt Carla should learn how to cook for him. Coming from a traditional, male-dominated household, he complained that his wife was "too bossy" and did not give him due respect. The more time Carla spent with his friends and family, the more clear it became that there was a real ethnic and cultural divide between them—in Raimundo's world the expectation was that the man, as head of the household, would be offered deference. Raised with a very different family structure, Carla expected a far more equal partnership and naturally rebelled against Raimundo's domination.

As time went on, other cultural differences became painfully divisive. In Raimundo's tradition, emotions were freely and frequently expressed. In Carla's world, conflict was avoided. When Carla would "clam up" and refuse to talk, let alone provide any sort of emotional response, Raimundo would become furious. For him this made it impossible to ever deal with a subject and put it behind them. As a result, he would vent, and the more he vented, the more Carla would withdraw.

For Carla's part, she was much too overwhelmed by Raimundo's rages and demands to continue in the relationship. Although she was willing to concede that his communication style was successful within the confines of his immediate family, she had no desire to join the fray.

In counseling it became clear that neither party was willing to adjust, nor had they taken the necessary time to consider the real differences in their cultural backgrounds and the potential impact of those differences on their day-to-day life together. Unwilling to compromise, they divorced.

Lessons to be learned from Carla and Raimundo:

- *"Marry in haste; repent at leisure."* Carla and Raimundo were proof of this old adage that transcends racial and cultural barriers. The sex is great, your mate is adorable, and the party is in your honor. Unfortunately, once the guests go home and the thank-you notes are sent, you're left with the day-to-day realities of a relationship. Even with real forethought and hard work, marriage is a tough proposition. Without that consideration, it's doomed more often than not and, even if the result isn't divorce, it can produce years of unnecessary misery.
- *It's not just what you say, it's how you say it.* Differences in communication styles as profound as Raimundo and Carla's can render what's actually being said a moot point. Each was so troubled by the other's manner of dealing with conflict that the conflicts themselves became almost secondary.
- *Simply understanding or respecting differences isn't enough.* Although his was nothing like her own family, Carla was able to see how Raimundo's family

could successfully communicate in a way very different from her own. That understanding did not translate into action because Carla had no desire to change her style of interaction.

- *Get to know your mate's family.* Family isn't always destiny, but it can be. Even if your mate doesn't want to duplicate his or her parent's marriage, he or she is certain to have picked up some cues from it. In the case of Raimundo, however, he was clearly happy and indeed expecting to carry on the traditional "macho" family structure. By rushing into marriage, the couple failed to consider what this would mean to them in the long term and ultimately went their separate ways.

Same Race, Different Culture

Just because you are both white or black or brown, there is no guarantee that your cultural expectations and experiences also match. This truth is painfully clear in the case of Martin and Kelsey.

Martin and Kelsey

Two People Who Were Apparently Similar, Yet Profoundly Different

When Martin and Kelsey became involved, their similarities seemed real predictors for a successful union. Both were married once before. Both had two early adolescent children for whom they were the primary caretakers. Their children had grown up knowing and liking each other. As a result, there were none of the typically encountered issues of trust between stepsiblings that we've discussed in other chapters. In fact, if it weren't for the very important, if not immediately apparent, differences in parental approach and expectations between Martin and Kelsey, the children would likely have lived together very successfully.

To understand what went wrong with this couple, it's necessary to know their histories. Martin was the child of Irish immigrants. His father went to work and, at the end of the day, came home and gave his paycheck to Martin's mother. To him, this fulfilled his paternal role in the family. Outside of performing "man's work" such as yard work and household repairs, Martin's father showed little interest in family life and no initiative in raising the children outside of delivering punishment as the children grew older and their infractions potentially serious. Although neither Martin nor his siblings got into any real trouble, the threat of "wait until your father gets home" was omnipresent. Neither unkind nor uncaring, Martin's father simply believed that the bulk of childrearing duties belonged to his wife, and as long as the bills were paid he was doing his share. Martin's mother went along with this arrangement and was the primary caretaker of her six children. Because they, too, were raised in the same manner, neither of Martin's parents questioned this rigid arrangement.

Martin met his first wife, Mary, while studying in Ireland. She came from a rural Irish family whose domestic arrangement mirrored that of Martin's parents. When the marriage began, Mary had every expectation of living her life just as Martin did, with her taking on the primary responsibility for the children and the home.

However, their relationship changed after the couple returned to the United States to marry and have children. For financial reasons, Mary had to work part-time. At first, she adhered to the traditional family structure, but eventually she began to become increasingly disenchanted with what she saw as the unfair burden of both working outside the home and being the family cook, chauffeur, and planner. Martin, however, continued to justify the status quo. He minimized Mary's part-time job because it involved fewer hours and was less physically taxing than his job working construction. He refused to help around the house or to hire help. When Mary attempted to delegate chores to their two sons, Martin objected because these tasks were not traditionally done by the boys in the family. He would get angry and accuse her of trying to make the boys sissies. Not surprisingly, the two divorced, and the boys went to live with their father, who promptly hired a housekeeper.

Kelsey's history was quite different. Kelsey's mother had five children and was widowed when the youngest was three. As a result, she had to go to work part-time and quickly became self-reliant. Kelsey's mom learned to do her own repairs, and her children of both sexes learned to pitch in and do whatever chores were necessary around the house. Having had to change her whole outlook on the sex-linked division of duties after her husband's death, Kelsey's mom became a firm believer in the idea that her sons as well as her daughters should know how to sew a button on and know how to cook for themselves. Age, physical capabilities, and intellectual capacity rather than gender became the determinants of who did what around the house.

Kelsey's first husband likely appealed to her because he professed both a desire and an ability to relieve her of the many daily chores with which she had been burdened from an early age. Unfortunately, it wasn't until two children and several years later that Kelsey was forced to accept that her husband's actions in no way matched his words. In their years together, he ran up a huge debt and established a relationship with another woman. During the messy divorce proceedings, which further depleted the family finances, Kelsey was awarded custody, and her husband essentially disappeared, leaving her, like her mother before her, alone to raise her children. At this juncture Kelsey decided to muster her resources and move on alone rather than put any more time or money into making her children's father take fiscal or emotional responsibility for them.

It was at this point in both their lives that Martin and Kelsey met. Unlike Carla and Raimundo, this couple did not deny the differences in their backgrounds and expectations. What they did do was put a spin on them that turned out to be far from realistic.

Martin and Kelsey examined their mutual histories and concluded that they were well suited to each other. Martin was good for her because he was financially responsible and wouldn't be running up debt. Kelsey could make Martin happy because she had demonstrated an ability to "do it all" while raising her children alone. In their minds the match would be ideal—Martin could stop paying a housekeeper, and Kelsey could stop worrying about the leaking sink and unmowed lawn. It seemed like the ideal solution.

Unfortunately, the devil (as is so often the case) was in the details. After the honeymoon stage was over, Kelsey thought nothing of asking one of Martin's boys, the first to arrive home every day, to defrost the evening's supper in the microwave or to do some other seemingly less-than-masculine chore. Consequently, an ever-increasing series of marital and family spats about the fair and reasonable division of labor ensued. The couple, truly good people who loved one another and had experienced significant guilt over the failures of their first marriages, made the decision to enter counseling.

During therapy, the first revelation came when Kelsey revealed she had come to realize she had actually married Martin's father. Martin, for his part, was generally puzzled as to why Kelsey wasn't grateful for the extra help she was getting; he believed he was making life much easier for her. Neither could understand why their children, who had started out getting along quite well, were now divided by their loyalties to their respective biological parents and were becoming increasingly unhappy and disruptive.

After the initial process of sorting through the situation, the couple began to see where, despite their genuine commitment, things began to go wrong and why it had happened so quickly. While each had developed skills as a single parent that seemed ideal for the other, the blend—which on the surface seemed like a sure thing—brought together hugely differing expectations. Further, it became clear to them that when they thought they had honestly addressed potentially divisive issues, in truth they had only addressed some of them and then in only the most positive and optimistic of ways.

After three months of marital counseling the couple arrived at a joint set of expectations that would work for them. Eventually they brought the children into the sessions, which allowed them to feel a part of the process and understand the new household rules. The children, who had started out liking each other in the first place, quickly adjusted to the new structure, aided by the fact that their parents provided consistent limits, generally supported one another, and learned to present themselves to the children as mature and loving parents.

Lessons to be learned from Kelsey and Martin:

- *Those who ignore history are doomed to repeat it.* As they did in their first marriages, Kelsey and Martin went into this second relationship with a rather black-and-white vision of how things would be and, again, had trouble dealing with the many gray areas that make up a relationship. Life is never simple, and a rigid expectation of how daily life will evolve is a blueprint for disaster.
- *Talk honestly about your views of male/female roles.* In this day and age it's easy to assume that the days of "women cook, men mow the lawn" are quaint and old-fashioned, but many of us subconsciously harbor fantasies of a traditional relationship. We all know the woman who married the handsome starving artist,

only to be furious he didn't rapidly morph into a successful provider. There's nothing wrong with traditional roles as long as both parties are happy to play them. If they go against your core beliefs, those beliefs will surface sooner or later, generally in a hostile form.

- *Children take their cues from their parents.* Even though these children basically liked each other, parental loyalties were (as they almost always are) the driving force behind their behavior. If you're unhappy and unclear about your relationship, you can be sure your children will be too, and that uncertainty will cause them to act out in a disruptive and rebellious manner.

- *You can work it out—if you want to.* With compromise and understanding of the forces that drive your behavior, change can happen if it's something both parties are invested in. The key is that it must be a joint effort; wishing won't make it so.

Religious Differences

Religious differences can come in two forms: people who were born of different faiths and people who have different approaches to the same faith (such as Orthodox versus Reform in the Jewish faith). While many people consider shared faith a vital component of marriage or remarriage, a rapidly increasing number marry outside of their theological background. In some cases one of the partners converts to the other's religion; in others a compact is made to honor both partners' traditions. In such cases the arrival of children may bring a previously smooth arrangement into a period of real conflict.

Some couples decide that although they share different beliefs the children will be raised in one faith or the other. In other instances, the children are exposed to the belief systems of both parents. Although this is the more democratic approach, it may serve to confuse the children about what their core beliefs should be or about the role that religion should play in their lives. To avoid such conflicts, some couples come together to select a new, neutral religious practice in which to raise their blended family.

Certainly the points of view on the subject of faith vary greatly and could be debated endlessly. In addition to those of faith, there are a number of families who have either no religious tradition or have abandoned the faith in which they were raised. What we'll address here are the issues that commonly arise in interfaith marriages.

Nothing stirs stronger emotions than issues of faith. Older people with grown children have been surprised to discover that their remarriage to a person of another theological bent can cause real problems with their adult offspring, even when those children are not active practitioners. Faith is greatly tied in to our family identity, and those who don't take its impact into consideration can be easily blindsided by the conflict that results. Although the couple must put themselves and their goals first, carefully considering the sentiments and feelings of other family members and treating them with respect will go a long way toward making the transition as smooth and happy as possible.

Mark and Julie

A Couple's Commitment to Marriage Means a Commitment to Faith

When Mark and Julie met, he was going through a difficult divorce. His first wife had been diagnosed with manic depression (a psychiatric disorder that takes the patient on mood swings from giddiness to despair) resulting in her being hospitalized on several occasions and in her inability to care for their six-year-old daughter, Jessica. Fortunately, Mark was a dedicated father who had been the primary caretaker, often acting as both mother and father, throughout the marriage and divorce. Both Mark and his first wife were observant members of the Jewish faith. Julie, on the other hand, was a nonpracticing Catholic.

Mark and Julie married. While Julie did not convert to Judaism, the couple comfortably raised their new son, Benjamin, in the Jewish faith. Meanwhile, little Jessica was thriving in the shared custody of both parents, and her transitions between households were generally smooth.

Mark had an astute understanding of his ex-wife's difficulties. Although medication and therapy had improved her condition, she was still at times unpredictable. Jessica was very responsive to Julie's stepparenting, which caused some resentment on the part of her biological mother. This resentment was exacerbated by the fact that Julie was a Catholic, which Jessica's mother made regular, negative comments about. This upset Jessica, who was quite fond of Julie. The result was tension between Julie and Mark.

The situation worsened when Jessica's mother decided to move to another community and, additionally, enrolled Jessica in a religious day-school program. According to Jessica's mother, the little girl was being unduly influenced by Julie's Catholicism and therefore needed more intensive religious training. To make matters worse, she expected Mark to pay for the school. Mark, who had his new family to support, along with child support and alimony, was already stretched financially thin, and tensions increased between him and Julie.

Committed to each other, Mark and Julie sought counseling. As a result Julie, who was no longer entrenched in her faith, made the decision to convert to Judaism. Once this process was complete, the comfort level between Julie and Jessica's mother improved. This religious transition was successful because of Julie's primary focus of faith: her relationship with Mark and her love for Benjamin and Jessica. Additionally, she had experienced a growing connection to Judaism and that, with her mostly lapsed Catholicism, made the decision to convert the right one for her.

Lessons to be learned from Julie and Mark:

- *Be clear about your commitment to faith.* From the outset, it was clear that Mark's commitment to his religious tradition was greater then Julie's and that they were both comfortable with that. However, had Julie felt a stronger connection to her Catholic upbringing, this situation would have been much harder to solve.

Religious conflicts can occur between members of the same faith as well as those of differing religious backgrounds. In these instances the two parties experience significant difficulties relating to the interpretation of specific religious traditions. A typical case in point is Sara and Michael.

Sara and Michael

How Commitment to Faith Can Sometimes Cause Conflict in a Blended Family

Sara and Michael were a Jewish couple who had grown up in the same town and were raised in a very similar tradition. They married right out of college after a courtship that began in midadolescence. For nine years things went well. They had three children. Eventually, however, Michael began to assume more responsibilities at work, which included a great deal of travel. The couple grew apart and eventually parted in a peaceful, if painful, divorce. Sara assumed primary custody of the children, and Michael had extremely liberal and flexible visitation.

After three years of this arrangement, Sara remarried. Morris, her new husband, was also Jewish but more observant. Under his influence Sara became more active in her faith and began to keep kosher for holidays. At the same time, Michael was moving further away from his faith. This was partially attributable to the fact that his parents had retired and moved to Florida, taking with them the holiday traditions and connection to religious ritual that kept Michael in touch with his Jewish heritage.

Small tensions began to arise between Sara and Michael as the children, who celebrated holidays as they always had, developed new traditions and expectations with the evolution of their mother's faith. Gradually, things grew more heated until they finally reached a boiling point at Passover when Rachel, their seven-year-old daughter, informed Michael she wouldn't eat from his dishes during Passover because they were "unclean." Michael was understandably hurt by this pronouncement and took his anger out on Sara and Morris, accusing them both of using religion to turn his children against him.

As so often happens, it was the children who paid the price for—and acted out as a result of—these escalating tensions. Their aggression increased as their ability to sleep and to pay attention decreased. Finally they were brought into counseling but without the participation of the parents and stepfather. However, when it was brought to the adults' attention that the root of the children's difficulties was in fact the difficulties among them, all three began active participation in the counseling process.

Things truly began to improve when, due to the nature of the conflict, the counselor suggested including a rabbi as part of the family's counseling/mentoring team. As a person vested with specific knowledge of religious traditions, the rabbi was able to offer expert council and reframe and mesh various traditions in a nonjudgmental manner.

The story of Sara and Michael shows how complex issues of religion can be. We can learn lessons from their situation:

- *Commitment to faith changes*. Even had Michael and Sara remained married, commitment to faith might have become an issue. When one party becomes more or less involved in religious observation, respect for the partner's (or former partner's) view is vital, particularly when children are involved. Too often one's manner of religious observation becomes linked with "right or wrong," and a child may feel he has to choose between the "good" or "bad" parent. While not rational, one can't help but understand that Michael probably felt his daughter was calling not just his plates but him "unclean." Tradition should be used to enhance the family, not to pit one side against the other, to denigrate those who have made a different choice, or to make a child exalt one parent over another.
- *In matters of faith, involve the clergy*. Whatever your conflict, you can rest assured your clergy member has seen it before. As a leader who deals with members of the temple/parish/mosque who worship daily as well as with those who make annual visits, he or she will likely have a far more objective view of the situation than either the lapsed practitioner or the newly fervent convert.
- *Children's behavior often reflects their parent's feelings*. Just because you don't yell and scream and pout doesn't mean your children aren't well aware that you'd probably like to. Lacking the constraints and perspectives of age, it's quite likely they'll act out the

frustrations, upset, and turmoil you're feeling. If your children suddenly exhibit a marked change in behavior, the first place to look for an explanation is at yourself.

Stuart and Rhonda

Confusing Loyalty to Family with Loyalty to Faith

Religious conflict is not always between current and former spouses. As we can see by Stuart's story, hurt feelings and conflict related to religion can affect extended family as well. Stuart and Lilly, both Episcopalian, met and married while in college. They had two children whom they raised together in the Episcopalian faith until Lilly was tragically killed in an automobile accident.

After Lilly's death, Stuart and the children remained very close to Lilly's parents and sisters, who were helpful in caring for the children after Lilly's death. Two years later, Stuart met and married a young Jewish woman, Rhonda. With this new addition to the family, Stuart and the children not only maintained their own religious tradition, but they began to incorporate some of Rhonda's cultural traditions as well. This angered Lilly's family, who became convinced this was merely the beginning of a plan by Rhonda to convert Stuart and the children entirely to Judaism.

Rhonda, however, had no such agenda. Unfortunately, Lilly's relatives made many unkind and angry comments in front of the children before Stuart and Rhonda were able to see the truth of the situation. Stuart discussed the situation in counseling and decided that if such remarks didn't stop, he would have to place limitations on the time the children spent with their grandparents. Ultimately a limit was set in a firm manner, and the grandparents—with a bit of distance and perspective over time—were able to realize that exposure to Judaism was respectful to Rhonda, not a disavowal of the religion practiced by their deceased child.

Stuart's story illustrates how easy it is to confuse issues of loyalty to faith and loyalty to family. Lessons to be learned from Stuart's situation:

- *For many, faith is an intrinsic part of identity.* The pain of losing a child is indescribable. For Lilly's parents, continuing the religious traditions she imparted to her children meant a continuation of their daughter's life. It may not have been right, but it is certainly not surprising that they experienced the incorporation of Rhonda's religion into the children's lives as a displacement of their daughter's legacy.
- *As a parent, you are in charge.* Certainly, Stuart understood his in-laws' pain. More important, however, was his primary commitment to keep his children from being hurt and confused by their grandparents' remarks. By setting limits, Stuart was able to instigate a cooling-off period that both protected the children from unnecessary vitriol and gave the grandparents time to see that their fears were unfounded.

What is clear in cases of racial, cultural, and religious differences is that you cannot move forward without addressing the past. The traditions we grew up with—good and bad—are bound to shape us and, if left unexamined, will likely if not unconsciously determine our future choices, for better or worse.

4

Blending Gay and Lesbian Families

AT ITS CORE, the ideal of marriage is a commitment between two people. Throughout modern history, however, that commitment had been morally and legally viewed as applicable only between two people of opposite gender. Most religious traditions view marriage as such. There is, however, a segment of society that believes that marriage can be viewed as a sexually bonded relationship, which seems to imply that the definition could be more broadly based to include same-sex relationships. The beginnings of a movement in this direction can be see by legislation recently enacted by the state of Vermont. The state passed legislation that recognizes unions between gays and lesbians as legitimate and confers to those couples benefits previously reserved exclusively for heterosexuals who were joined in traditional or common-law marriage.

It seems increasingly likely that wide-ranging legal decisions in this direction are imminent. Yet despite the law, cultural tradition and deeply felt religious dogma do not change easily. Therefore, it is unlikely that these types of domestic partnerships will be widely accepted any time soon.

In the meantime, there are any number of purportedly heterosexual, "traditional" marital partnerships in which one or even both partners are either bisexual or gay/lesbian. Often these marriages endure in order to present a politically and/or religiously correct facade to the world. Often the "normal," traditional marriage is continued with the understanding that one or both of the spouses may pursue homosexual relations outside of marriage. In some cases the straight partner is unaware of the gay partner's proclivities, and, indeed, the gay partner may have long denied his or her longings in order to live a "normal" life. Finally, there are instances where one or the other partner had his or her first sexual experience or attraction to a member of the same sex only after years of a heterosexual lifestyle. These people should not be thought of as converts. Rather, they should be recognized as people who took some time to find the person who unequivocally awakened feelings that until that point may have been vague, uncertain, uncomfortable, and easy to ignore without a specific person to attach them to.

Although adults may learn to cope with any of these situations— albeit painfully and with difficulty—the issue clearly becomes far more complex and volatile when children are involved.

Assessing how and when to try and introduce these issues of alternative sexuality to a child is a difficult but important and worthwhile process. If you consider the normal patterns of childhood development and how children react to change and stress, it is easy to conclude that adolescence is probably the single most difficult time to announce any changes in the family structure. In the final analysis, the earlier you can make a child aware of a parent's sexual identity, the better. Barring an early revelation, waiting until adulthood—if circumstances permit— might be the prudent choice. However, given the option between telling an adolescent the truth and concocting an elaborate deception, truth is the best option. Painful as it might be, it's sure to be less destructive than a web of lies that can lead to a lifetime of trust issues.

When considering whether to reveal the truth of a parent's sexuality, or indeed any other potentially traumatic information, it is useful to note this important fact: children generally make a far better postseparation/postdivorce adjustment after the end of a chaotic marriage than they do after the dissolution of a seemingly placid union that ends for no reason apparent to them.

Clearly this indicates the importance of letting children know, within a developmentally appropriate framework, what issues were involved in the divorce. In addition, any child faced with potentially traumatic information and change can, as stated previously, benefit greatly from the opportunity to receive professional and neutral therapeutic help, either individually or with the family unit. Children often need reassurance that they are not responsible for problems between their parents, that they are, in fact, OK. Additionally, when issues of sexual identity are involved in a parental rift, children—particularly those in or near adolescence—will frequently question and have concerns about their own sexuality.

Steven

Don't Underestimate a Child's Emotional Reaction to an Amicable Separation

Steven was nine years old when he first came to therapy as a result of complaints about his bad behavior both at home and at school, particularly his resistance to parental authority. While these problems may not seem unique, his family dynamic made them so.

Steven had two younger brothers, ages six and three. He lived in an intact home with two loving parents. However, although the parents had begun their life together in a mutually heterosexual union, each of them came to realize over time that they were in fact both bisexual. As a result, each partner developed a stable, same-sex relationship outside of the marriage. Nonetheless, they continued to live together for some time before mutually deciding that, given the long-term nature of both affairs, a separation—if not a divorce—made sense.

Steven's father decided that he should be the one to move out. He moved in with his boyfriend in an apartment near the family home. After this transition took place, the mother's girl-friend moved in with her and the children. Prior to this living arrangement, both of the parents' new mates had had positive contact with the children. After the move, Steven's dad continued to provide financial support devoid of any legal action compelling him to do so. The children continued to have regular contact with their father and his partner at their new home.

On the surface, everything was open and aboveboard. The arrangement seemed to satisfy all parties involved. Indeed, the younger children were taking it in stride, as much as a child would any such disruption. Steven, however, was another matter. Although he appeared to be handling things in much the same manner as the younger children, in truth he was undergoing a huge internal struggle in response to the massive changes going on around him. His behavioral difficulties were a direct result of this struggle.

The adults in his life had quite wrongly assumed that because he had a positive connection to all of the grown-ups involved in this complicated situation, all would be well. They assumed that if they worked together to make the transitions smooth, there would be no necessity to involve Steven in the details. This was the wrong assumption. Steven was old enough to need to be involved, not to mention that he required reassurance that the new circumstances were about the desires and attachments of his parents and in no way any fault of his.

Once the parents were brought in to the therapy sessions for the purpose of full disclosure, Steven was able to begin to clearly understand what was happening. When the boy was able to comprehend that none of what was going on was directly related to his behavior, his attitudes and actions improved dramatically. In the final breakthrough, Steven expressed curiosity about his own sexual identity. He ultimately admitted that he had been aware of his parents' respective sexual orientations long before they told him the facts themselves. What made all the difference in Steven's life was that finally everyone began to talk honestly about the changes in the family, as opposed to going on as usual and avoiding the proverbial elephant that was clearly in the middle of the room.

Lessons to be learned from Steven's story:

- *Children are highly aware of things, even if you think they aren't.* Attempting to hide the truth from children is ultimately futile. It often leads to unhappiness and confusion on the part of the children, who will often take this lack of disclosure as a cue that they are responsible if they are not included in the real reasons for a family dissolution.
- *All children are not alike.* Age, temperament, and stage of development—all of these factor into what a child should be told in any situation. For Steven's younger siblings, the fact that their parents seemed happy and they had regular contact with adults they loved was enough. For Steven, whose development and cognitive abilities were far greater than the younger children's, this offering of the new situation as a happy fait accompli was simply not appropriate.
- *Children are aware of sexuality even if adults are not comfortable thinking about it.* By ignoring a child's sexual awareness, parents at best confuse her and at worst may lead her to believe that her interest and concerns are "dirty" or "wrong." Suit the conversation to the child's developmental level, but don't ignore the topic altogether. Additionally, don't be worried that a child's interest in sexuality will result in her acting out in a way inappropriate to her years. Unless improperly and abusively exposed to sexuality, children's explorations and questions are innocent, natural, and nothing that should cause concern or rebuke.

Karyn and Linda

Honesty and Communication Ease the Process of Family Restructuring

Although most situations involving the blending of gay or lesbian families are rife with problems, some people have a gift for handling them just right to the betterment of all concerned. Two such role models are Karyn and Linda, a lesbian couple who managed a happy household with two children from previous heterosexual marriages, who—thanks to their thoughtful care—grew up emotionally strong and healthy to deal with potentially difficult situations.

Karyn had married at the age of twenty-one and had one son, Daniel. She divorced at the age of twenty-nine. During her marriage, she experienced conflict and eventually came to realize that her sexual inclination was toward women. She fell in love with another woman, and her marriage ended. Karyn retained joint custody of her son with her former husband, with whom she had as she described a "mature custody arrangement." In other words, both she and her ex-husband shared the belief that Daniel's interests had to come first. Karyn and her lover bought a home together, despite knowing in their hearts that the relationship was not a permanent one, and, indeed, after three years the two women separated. Karyn lived on her own for the next five years. Daniel spent his weeks with her and his weekends with his father, who remarried at about the time Karyn and her lover parted. Daniel's father eventually had two more children.

Things went smoothly for some time. When Daniel was eleven, he was told the truth about his mother's sexuality, a truth he had long suspected. In the next year, Karyn became involved with Donna, and this instigated the first significant stress in the relationship between Karyn and her former spouse. For reasons that never became clear to her, he suddenly displayed a great deal of anger and in fact sought sole custody of Daniel on two separate occasions. Interestingly, Daniel, who had developed into an exceptionally bright and articulate adolescent, remarked on more than one occasion that Karyn and Donna's relationship was better than that of his father and stepmother.

Karyn and Donna maintained their relationship for thirteen years and remained close friends after their love affair ended. Each woman had a different view of her own sexual orientation. Donna had been aware that she was a lesbian since early adolescence. Karyn, however, had not considered a same-sex love affair until her late twenties and never ruled out the possibility of being attracted to another man.

Karyn then became involved with Linda. Karyn and Linda had been friends for many years before becoming partners. With this relationship, both women feel that they have finally met the person with whom they will spend the rest of their lives. When discussing the issues involved in blending a family, Karyn expressed the view that, in her experience, blending involved restructuring the family, a vision shared by Linda. They also agreed that a vital component of successful blending is viewing themselves as not just a couple but as part of a larger family. The final union of Linda and Karyn was the result of years of counseling that helped them to develop open and honest communication and a genuine understanding of the importance of family stability. They reviewed not only their emotional issues but also their environment, choosing to live in a very liberal community where many lifestyles are accepted. They based their family decisions on the needs of their children.

The example of Karyn and Linda is one of real maturity along with realistic behaviors and expectations. Lessons to be learned from their situation:

- *Focus on the well-being of the children involved.* Be open and honest with them. Don't concern yourself simply with what makes you happy as a couple, but focus on the family as a whole.
- *Choose your environment.* Karyn and Linda lived in a progressive community where their lifestyle was generally accepted. When possible, choose an environment where alternative lifestyles do not automatically mean that you and your children are ostracized.

Andrea and Sophia

Same-Sex Relationships Can Create Tensions Beyond the Immediate Family ·

Andrea and Sophia were a lesbian couple who had been together for three years. Each had a daughter from a previous marriage: Andrea's daughter was fourteen, Sophia's seventeen. Both girls had boyfriends, and Andrea and Sophia got along well with both boyfriends.

When the parents of the fourteen-year-old's boyfriend discovered that Andrea was gay, they forbade their son to date her. As a result, the young couple was forced to sneak time together, and Andrea's daughter eventually became pregnant. This event brought Andrea and her daughter to treatment.

Unfortunately, no close relationship was ever established between the baby boy and his father and paternal grandparents, who provided financial support but no contact. Over time, and with the help of a counselor, Andrea and her daughter were able to accept the choice of the father and his family and refrain from taking responsibility for behavior and attitudes over which they had no control. This allowed them to move on with life.

Andrea helped raise her grandson, and when he turned seven, her daughter married a man who became the boy's adoptive father after his biological father willingly gave away his rights.

While offering no hard-and-fast solutions, Andrea and Sophia's story reminds us that people do not live in a vacuum. This in no way suggests anyone should live a lie, but it's important to anticipate the potential consequences of revealing the truth.

Alma and Charles

Harmonious Blending of Families of Same-Sex Couples Is Certainly Possible

Alma and Charles married and had one child, Elizabeth. Several years into marriage, Alma came to the realization that she was a lesbian. Still, the marriage ended amicably, with Alma and Charles remaining good friends who focused on the best interests of their child. Elizabeth adapted well and enjoyed a good relationship with both parents.

Charles eventually remarried and had two more sons. Alma also found a partner with whom she established a permanent relationship through a commitment ceremony (albeit not a legally sanctioned one). Both new partners accepted Elizabeth and their mates' former spouses. Elizabeth grew up happy and well adjusted and went on to law school. While she was there, Alma broke up with her mate and reattached to a new woman with two children of her own. Because of her happy upbringing, Elizabeth was able to accept this new development in her family structure.

While this may not seem to apply to most families, the knowledge that peaceful and thoughtful resolutions can be achieved should offer hope to those in the midst of a more contentious situation. It also serves to remind us that sexual orientation is no indicator of the ability—or lack thereof—to resolve complicated family dynamics in a mature and thoughtful manner.

What dynamics allowed these families to blend so well?

- Charles and Alma liked and respected one another as people and trusted one another's parenting. They also knew that they could and would maintain good boundaries.
- Everyone involved was bright, communicative, and self-assured of his or her own identity. When conflicts arose, they were able to talk things out.
- These people wanted to get on with their own lives. Open-mindedness and a desire to embrace the future rather than a need to cling to the past enabled this lucky family group to have a peace rarely experienced by gay or straight couples.

Elaine and Susan

Role-Playing Issues Affect All Couples

As the story of Elaine and Susan illustrates, same-sex couples are plagued with identity and role-playing issues much as heterosexual couples are.

Elaine and Susan came to awareness of their sexual orientation at different times in their lives. Elaine discovered her sexuality in her twenties, while Susan was aware of her sexuality since puberty. When the two formed a partnership, neither had been previously married nor involved in a long-term commitment. Both had thriving careers, but Susan's was the more high-powered and lucrative. When they wanted to have children, they decided that Elaine would undergo in vitro fertilization. Indeed, the couple went on to have three children in this way. Both were active parents, but Elaine took on the role of primary caretaker, and, as in a traditional male/female household, Elaine regularly sacrificed her own needs for her family. While things looked good on the surface, trouble was brewing underneath.

One growing problem was the lack of a male role model in their son's life. He began to exhibit behavioral problems, both at home and at school. At the same time, Elaine began to struggle with ambivalent feelings about being the family's primary caregiver, a role she had played for most of her life. Additionally, she increasingly felt that Susan didn't appreciate her, and, as a result, her self-esteem was rapidly diminishing.

Outside intervention in the form of both individual and couples therapy became necessary. It was only when they became involved in this process that the women were able to realize that their issues were "normal" ones that frequently occur among couples regardless of sexual orientation. They learned that their problems were not a special set of circumstances resulting from their nontraditional union.

In addition to seeking professional help for themselves, it became apparent to both parents that their son, Brian, also needed assistance. Initially they dealt with a school counselor with whom Brian was able to openly discuss his difficulties. That counselor sent them to an outside therapist whom all three were receptive to. Between the outside therapist and the school counselor, Brian began to feel less conflicted about his life. As both counselors were male, they offered Brian some of the balance he needed. Additionally, they provided some useful guidance to Elaine and Susan, including the suggestion of a Big Brother for Brian. During that time the couple reevaluated their own relationship, and Susan began to participate more fully in family life, a change of pattern that she ultimately found very rewarding.

Lessons to be learned from Elaine and Susan's story

- *The role of the family caretaker, regardless of gender, is an extremely stressful one.* It is incumbent upon other family members—and the person in the caretaker role—to be aware of this. The primary caretaker deserves respect and support and must learn to expect and ask for it when it's not forthcoming.
- *At their core, most human experiences are universal.* Assuming an experience is unique to you and your family makes it difficult, if not impossible, to obtain the objectivity necessary to cope. The more you can see yourself in others, the more you'll be able to step back and consider different coping strategies. Understanding that you're not the only one in a given situation can lessen stress and ease tensions so that the parties involved can move forward.
- *Children, whether they or their parents are straight or gay, need same-sex role models with whom they can share gender-related experiences and form a vision of themselves in their future.*

As gays and lesbians become increasingly visible, vested, and accepted in mainstream society, the blending of same-sex and traditional families will also increase. As people begin to understand that they are more the same than different, the chances for raising healthy, happy, and accepting children in these new families will increase. Although opponents of gay and lesbian parenting frequently voice concern that such situations are "bad for the children," research has shown that children who have loving and stable homes are highly likely to thrive, despite their parents' sexual orientation.

5

Blending Families with a History of Physical, Sexual, or Emotional Abuse

BLENDING A FAMILY under the best of circumstances can be a complex and difficult process, but when previous family experiences include abuse, the participants must exercise extreme caution and patience when bringing this new unit together. Any human being who has been abused or neglected by a parent, spouse, or primary caretaker will have severe difficulty developing trusting relationships. This is especially true if the victim-abuser relationship was one of consistent closeness and interdependence. A young child who has experienced such horrors has little reason to believe that any other type of relationship is possible, and he will generally act out in rather predictable patterns.

Behavioral Tendencies of Abused Children

After being sexually exploited, some children come to believe that their only personal worth is directly tied to their bodies. Rather than shy away from sexuality and contact, they may present themselves in a way that is surprisingly—and unnervingly—seductive. It is important that adults firmly reject any sexual overtures while resisting the natural reaction of becoming angry or upset, which will only add to the perception that abused children frequently have: that they are to blame for what happened to them. Strictly defined and consistently enforced boundaries are vital in such situations. These children need to learn that they can be valued for their thoughts, feelings, and nonsexual actions.

Another common tendency among children who have been sexually or physically abused is to divide the world into two camps—victim and aggressor. Because being a victim feels bad, the child chooses the role of the aggressor and may attempt to perpetrate abuse upon other younger and more vulnerable victims—sometimes animals, sometimes other children. Before an abused child can be safely brought into a new living situation with other children, the potential for such behavior must be explored and either ruled out or dealt with. Ignoring such potentialities could be disastrous. Instead, confront these issues in a forthright manner. Set very clear boundaries and behavioral expectations for all of the children involved. Outline what behavior is acceptable and what is inappropriate. Never assume that an abused child knows the difference, particularly if the abuse has been chronic. Children learn from their caregivers, and these children have had their behavior modeled by a person completely lacking in boundaries, to whom the most inappropriate and abusive behavior is entirely acceptable.

In rarer instances a child who has suffered genuine abuse may go on to make false allegations against others as a way of projecting blame for what happened to him. This behavior is extraordinarily difficult to manage and should always lead to a thorough clinical assessment and therapeutic treatment by a specialist in such matters.

Sadly, sometimes the pattern of abuse occurs throughout a series of parental partnerships and familial blendings and dissolutions. This is generally the result of adults failing to address and work through their own issues of self-esteem, past abuse, addictions, or mental illness. As a result they move from one destructive relationship to another, dragging their children with them.

Frequently, in cases of chronic abuse, children develop posttraumatic behavioral changes including flashbacks (recurrent mental images or memories of the traumatic event or events). Such behaviors are frequently triggered by change, even if the change is a positive one. Therefore, when undertaking such activities as a move, a change in schools, or the addition of a new member to the family, it is important to be prepared for some regression in behavior—fear, acting out, bed-wetting, or the like—on the part of the child with a history of abuse.

Abuse is not only sexual or physical. A parental figure who is consistently neglectful or uninvolved can damage a child as surely as a fist can. Children in these situations suffer from low self-esteem and a general mistrust of others. They can also be masters at testing the new people in their lives because they see themselves as essentially unlovable. Here again, the issues of trust for the child must be addressed with patience, consistency, and a loving but firm set of boundaries and limits.

Children with any history of abuse commonly put the new adults in their lives through a lengthy and difficult period of testing limits. Generally the child chooses one of two styles of dealing with newcomers. The first is to reject the new adult in a blunt and obvious manner. This behavior results from the child's certainty that he will ultimately be rejected, and so, by rejecting first, he is able in his mind to exert at least some control over the situation. Alternatively, the child may engage in a lengthy and confusing battle with the new adult. This behavior involves accepting the newcomer one minute and rejecting him or her the next in a roller coaster of behavior and emotions that, again, allows him to at least feel that he is in control of who is and isn't included in his day-to-day life.

When blending family members with a background of abuse, the parents must prepare themselves to deal with the difficulties of both extreme acting out and more covert passive aggression. Not unexpectedly, the child is generally anticipating abuse or neglect from the new person in his life. After all, his own guardian hurt him—why should you be any different?

In the home environment, parents can take steps to ensure that there is the appropriate privacy, space, and parental monitoring and oversight for all family members. This becomes paramount when there is the possibility that one child might enact abuse on other children in the family. Boundaries can be violated with younger children under the guise of playing games. The abused child has likely learned all about coercion and will mirror the behavior of his abuser by coercing others into keeping quiet, making them feel that they have done wrong or that they or their loved ones will be in real danger if the secret is revealed.

Finally, children in almost all abusive situations live with the fear that if their situation is revealed, they will lose their loved ones either as a result of being removed from the home or because of threats of physical harm. These fears can persist long after children have ceased to have contact with their abusers, as the story of Rose and Tom illustrates.

Rose and Tom

An Abusive Parent Undermines a New Family

When they first met, both Rose and Tom had been divorced for a number of years, and both were the parents of young teens. They dated for some time during which both sets of children seemed to approve of their relationship. That changed, however, when the couple announced plans to marry. Rose's children did an abrupt about-face and became very sullen. They began to act out in school and at home and, in particular, directed their hostilities toward Tom, whom they appeared to like and trust up until that point. After five months of worsening behavior and a decision to postpone the wedding, treatment was sought. After several months of therapy, the reason for the children's distress was revealed: Rose's first husband, a batterer, had told their sons that he would kill their mother should she ever remarry. Once this horrible secret was out in the open, the combined action of legal intervention and intervention by the therapist allowed the boys to feel safe and comfortable enough to move into the new family relationship and allow the marriage to take place.

Lessons to be learned from Rose and Tom:

- *Batterers are experts at instilling fear*. Don't assume that just because the abuser is out of the picture, his threats are, too. An abuser has a unique gift for

survival, and control over his or her victims is a vital
component in the ability to continue the abusive
behavior.
- *Children keep secrets.* Chances are no matter how
much a child has revealed, there are still things he has
yet to tell you. Assume you've heard only part of the
story and keep an open ear—sudden changes in
behavior indicate that there's more to the story. Make
it safe for the child to tell the whole tale.

The simple fact of abuse—sexual, physical, or emotional—does
not guarantee a child will be glad or grateful that his parents have separated. Children are as capable as anyone else of clinging to a fantasy
of what might be, as the story of Jack and Marjorie shows us.

Jack and Marjorie

Abused Children Who Idealize Their Family

Jack and Marjorie were married for eleven years. Jack, who
suffered from manic-depressive illness, was both unpredictable
and emotionally abusive throughout the union. The marriage
produced two children, Brett and Sarah, who were eight and
six, respectively, at the time of the divorce. Marjorie retained
custody of the children, who continued visitation with their
father, albeit on a rather inconsistent schedule. The time Jack
did spend with his children frequently caused them distress, as
his behavior continued to be unpredictable and sometimes
emotionally abusive.

Despite his father's behavior, Brett was unable to accept
the possibility of his mother becoming involved with someone
new. He entered therapy to deal with postdivorce issues. The

primary focus of these sessions was Brett's belief that if his parents reunited, everything would be fine. Throughout these sessions, Brett was able to confront the reality of his father's illness and the impact that it had on him. Finally, he was able to see the situation clearly so that he could move forward and allow his mother to do the same.

Lessons to be learned from Jack and Marjorie:

- *Children love their parents unconditionally.* That may seem like a simple fact, but in truth it is a complex and sometimes minimized factor in building any new family relationship or dissolving an old one. A child's love causes him to see the parental figure in the best possible light. It keeps alive the hope that this parent, no matter how genuinely unfit, might one day become the ideal father or mother.
- *Everyone harbors fantasies of the ideal family.* Like all people, children want to think only the best of their loved ones. It's a mistake to assume that children can't be conflicted between wanting to be with a loved one and wanting a loved one's bad behavior to stop— anyone who's ever been in an unhappy love affair can understand and attest to that impulse.

Kurt and Jill

A Parent's Own History of Abuse Resurfaces in a Time of Stress

Kurt and Jill were a lovely young couple who met while in college and dated for three years before marrying. Kurt was from the Midwest, Jill from the deep South. As time progressed they decided to become parents. Within three years of that decision they became the parents of three children, twin boys and a neurodevelopmentally delayed infant daughter who required constant care.

Jill, who had always seemed easygoing, suddenly became impulsive and occasionally aggressive when dealing with the twins, who were at a highly active stage of development. Baffled by his wife's seemingly atypical behavior, Kurt confronted her. Only then did Jill reveal the horrors of her own childhood: she had been physically abused by her father. Both she and her sister were regularly taken out to the woodshed and severely beaten for merely behaving as active children.

Jill was horrified by her own behavior and came to realize that her actions—while not as brutal—directly mimicked those of her father. Even though she recognized and was horrified by her own behavior, it was difficult for her to learn how to stop acting out. On some level, she began to identify with her aggressor in order to no longer be a victim of her situation.

Clearly the combination of her own unresolved experiences of abuse coupled with the strains of raising her rambunctious twins and ailing infant called up some learned, primitive responses to stress.

Lessons to be learned from Kurt and Jill:

- *You can't escape your past.* If you have a history that includes emotional, physical, or sexual abuse, it must be dealt with. If not, the effects will eventually surface, often when you're too overwhelmed by events to deal with them. It's normal to feel rage, even the desire to punish, after experiencing such horrors. The important thing is to deal with those angry urges with the help of a trained therapist before you find yourself taking them out on someone you love.

- *Abuse is insidious.* Like a faulty gene, abuse passes its horrors from generation to generation. It takes only one person to stop the cycle. Maybe it's you.

A history of abuse in no way precludes the possibility that a family can be successfully blended. However, all the participants must proceed carefully and thoughtfully and be willing to build trust and affection over time.

In the next chapter, we'll deal with a situation common to children who are abused or neglected by their parents—being placed in the care of their grandparents.

6

Grandparents and the Blended Family

FOR MOST ADULTS, memories of our time with grandparents are happy ones. From our first fishing lesson to that extra cookie before dinner, grandparents offer a loving refuge where a grandchild can do little wrong. Unfortunately, that ideal isn't true for everyone. For some, a battle for control between parents and grandparents may mean the relationship offers more conflict than comfort. For others whose parents are unable to care for them, the grandparent assumes the role of parent, with all of the resultant complications.

The Custodial Grandparent

In addition to the support role grandparents play in many families, an increasing number of older adults are bringing their grandchildren into their homes and raising them. Although this dynamic is not new, the numbers are. According to statistics gathered by the U.S. Census Bureau, in 1990 there were 3.9 million children living with their grandparents. In 1970, the figure for children in the same situation was 2.2 million. Why the 76 percent increase? There are a number of reasons.

Younger grandparents frequently find themselves caring for the offspring of a teenage pregnancy. An increase in substance abuse and HIV/AIDS-related illness among parents has also been a major contributing factor. An increasing awareness and reportage of child abuse and the state's intervention in and removal of children from such dangerous situations are others. Last, an increasing number of parents are incarcerated, many on drug-related charges.

The statistics compiled on such situations also reveal that the challenges faced by grandparents who are in effect raising a second family are tremendous. For one, many grandparents raising their grandchildren sustain financial difficulties. They are 60 percent more likely to live in poverty than grandparents who don't have the same responsibilities. They are also prone to neglecting their own physical and emotional needs in favor of those of the children, and most of these children tend to experience a higher degree of specialized needs due to trauma of abuse, neglect, parental separation, and possibly abandonment.

Grandparents who find themselves in this situation have another common burden to bear—most are torn between loving and wanting the best for their grandchildren and feeling that their own children have taken advantage of them. Frequently they feel cheated out of their retirement years as well as the fun of being the indulgent grandparent rather than the boundary-setting primary caretaker. As a result, resentments can fester. Of course, this situation is not always the result of their grandchildren being left in their care. In some cases, parents did not choose to turn their children over to their own parents but were forced to do so due to state intervention, sometimes at the grandparents' behest. These cases are messy and painful for everyone involved.

Sal and Maria

Proactive Parenting Across Generations

Sal and Maria were a recently retired couple, both sixty-five years of age. They had been married for forty-two years and were the parents of three children, all girls, who had given them seven grandchildren among them. While two of the daughters were in stable, happy marriages, their youngest, Rita, was drug and alcohol dependent. Although she had never been in a long-term relationship, she had given birth to two children, whose fathers' identities she claimed not to know.

Rita's two girls, ages six and eight, were taken from their mother by local child guardianship authorities as a result of neglect and drug abuse in the presence of the children. Social services contacted Sal and Maria, who agreed to have the girls placed in their care. At first, the arrangement was informal, but after a short time Sal and Maria found it necessary to obtain legal guardianship in order to have control over the girls' medical care and enroll them in the local school. What might have been a relatively simple process became expensive and time-consuming because Rita objected to her parents assuming these rights. Rita, unemployed and indigent, was entitled to free legal assistance, but Sal and Maria ended up spending thousands of dollars for the right to care for and support their grandchildren. When the legal wrangling finally ended, Sal and Maria gained guardianship, and Rita had weekly supervised visitation in their home.

Despite having fought for custody of their grandchildren, Sal and Maria's fervent hope was that Rita would get the help she needed and assume proper parental responsibility for the girls. Unfortunately, Rita continued her drug use. At first her older sisters and their husbands tried to help, but her erratic behavior and threats from one of her many boyfriends caused them to pull away, leaving Sal and Maria isolated and worn out from the difficult situation.

Sal and Maria were not accustomed to looking outside the family for help. However, when the girls began to act out in school and suffer nightmares and incidents of bed-wetting, they turned to their parish priest for help. Well acquainted with the various troubles and needs of his parishioners, the priest immediately connected them with a local mental health clinician who was experienced in dealing with children from neglectful situations.

The therapist's first goal was to help Sal and Maria stop blaming themselves for Rita's behavior. Once they were able to get past their guilt, they could set firmer and more consistent limits. With more structure in their lives, the girls felt safer and more in control and, as a result, began to act out less. For a brief period, family life seemed to settle down. Unfortunately, this new calm didn't last long.

Not long after things began to improve, Rita overdosed on drugs and died. Sadly, time away from parental responsibilities had not been enough to help her take charge of her life. After their mother's death, the girls continued to live with their grandparents but spent increasing amounts of time with one of their aunts and her family. Over time, plans were made, both socially and legally, to transfer the care of the girls to this aunt and uncle should anything happen to the grandparents. This plan arranged for the orderly and predictable transfer of the girls to their new caregivers should it become necessary. Indeed, when their grandmother passed away eight years after they first arrived in her home, that is exactly what happened.

Lessons to be learned from Sal and Maria:

- *A drug-dependent parent may never recover and resume his or her responsibilities.* Not surprisingly, Sal and Maria were invested in the notion that their daughter would pull herself together. As a result, the chaos of Rita's life transferred to their own.
- *Legal arrangements are necessary for children to be properly protected and cared for.* Aside from the practicalities of school and medical care, children need certainty in their living arrangements, and caregivers must protect both themselves and the youngsters from an erratic parent who tries to regain control by showing up and removing the children from the home.
- *Children need boundaries.* It's not unusual for a grandparent's guilt to translate into indulgence of inappropriate behavior. This doesn't do children any favors. They need positive structure, structure that

was doubtless desperately lacking with their addicted/abusive parent. If you want children to feel safe and begin to settle into a normal pattern, you must provide the limits in which they can flourish.

- *Plan for the future.* Clearly, the older the caregiver, the greater the potential for illness or death and the possibility of having to make another living arrangement for the minors involved. Involving the children as much as possible in the lives of other relatives or potential caregivers will minimize the trauma that likely accompanied their first transition.

- *Get help. Grandparents will find a very different set of circumstances involved in rearing grandchildren as opposed to raising their own children.* Children face different issues than they did a generation ago. Among these issues are a higher incidence of sexual activity among teens and violence in schools. More benign issues like the use of computers and video games—activities that are common to kids but probably foreign to grandparents—could make the all-important monitoring of these activities difficult if not impossible. Whether it's a counselor who can help you talk with children or a technologically savvy neighbor who can teach you to surf the Internet, outside assistance is vital to understanding the world your grandchildren live in.

James and Jessica

Children Who Become Parents Themselves

When teenager Jessica became pregnant by her boyfriend, James, her own parents threw her out. James's parents, Agnes and Tony, however, opted to take in the young couple and their child.

Initially, things went well. James's mother baby-sat while Jessica and James simultaneously worked toward completing their education—she in high school and he in community college. Tensions mounted after Jessica became pregnant a second time. James was angry because they had agreed not to have more children until he had completed school and saved some money. Jessica, for her part, denied responsibility for the pregnancy, which created a great deal of tension not only for the couple but between Jessica and James's family as well. Increasingly, there was a sense that Jessica had "worn out her welcome," but should she and the children leave the family home a custody battle would ensue. (The grandparents were hoping that she would simply leave and they would raise the children.)

Fortunately, the family avoided this battle after Jessica admitted what everyone had suspected: she had not followed the agreed-upon birth control plan and was indeed responsible for the pregnancy. To her, the additional child meant a "complete" family, one that would enable her and James to settle down into a stable life. Once she was able to get past her fear and admit the truth, James could forgive her, and the family could begin to address issues of trust and responsibility. As therapy progressed, Jessica began to understand that it was OK to be her own person and that having different ideas and concerns from the family who "took her in" in no way meant that she didn't love or respect them.

As the couple matured, their roles and the roles of Agnes and Tony became more clearly defined. James and Jessica functioned more as an independent couple, and the grandparents learned to be more accepting of their growing family and more empowering when interacting with them. For example, Agnes learned that the family functioned more effectively when she stopped getting up for midnight feedings and allowed Jessica to assume her rightful maternal role. Agnes and Tony learned to let go of the notion that they had a great deal to say about how the young people conducted their lives as a result of being their "rescuers."

Lessons to be learned from James and Jessica:

- *Don't abandon your children. Everyone makes mistakes.* Unless their behavior is violent or destructive to other family members, teenagers are still children who need all the support they can get. If unable to find stable employment or housing, young people can deteriorate quickly on their own. Sex may become the only way they can find to support themselves, drugs their only means of escape. It's one thing to make children take responsibility; it's another to force them into a situation that could escalate into paying a far higher price. James's parents offered compassion, and both youngsters responded by responsibly pursuing work and education.
- *When there's sex, there's a potential for pregnancy.* This may seem obvious, but James and his parents never fully addressed this reality. Jessica may have abdicated her birth control responsibilities, but James was equally responsible for both pregnancies. When grandparents, or anyone, permit a couple to continue a sexual relationship under their roof, they run the risk of adding to the household. Addressing this issue and its consequences before another baby is conceived is much more useful than finger pointing after the fact. Also, don't give the male a pass simply because he's not the one carrying a child. If he can father a child, he can buy a condom.
- *There's a fine line between supporting and enabling.* While Jessica and James were making strides toward maturity in the form of education and employment, they were still children in the family home. Many

parents, not eager for their youngsters to leave the nest, are secretly happy to keep them dependent, even while they may make a show of complaining about their dependent offspring. You owe it to your children to help them grow up with the ultimate goal of living independent and productive lives.

Ann and Mike

Grandparents Who Provided a Transition

Grandparent custody arrangements do not have to be permanent. When a grandparent works with a willing parent toward the goal of reuniting the parent and the child in an autonomous home, the results can be highly successful.

Ann and Mike decided to take in their four-year-old grandson, Aaron, when the relationship between their struggling daughter Pamela and her boyfriend, Jerry, became abusive. Jerry and Pamela had been together for six years, but over time Jerry, eight years Pamela's senior, had become increasingly controlling and aggressive.

Aaron began to manifest the effects of witnessing domestic violence. Pamela, who had been unable to leave Jerry for her own sake, found the strength to do it for her son. Yet this positive step left her physically and emotionally depleted with a habit of poorly and inconsistently disciplining Aaron.

Fortunately, Pamela was able to see the wisdom in her parents' offer to become Aaron's primary caretakers. This would give her space and enable her to attend individual and group counseling on domestic violence issues as well as complete job training to become self-sufficient. Pamela visited with Aaron and her parents on a regular basis and maintained a close relationship with her son. As she became stronger, she took him for day, then weekend, visits.

When Pamela was ready to resume a full-time parenting role, Aaron had adjusted to her new parenting style and ability to function in the world as a mature and independent adult.

Ann and Mike were pleased with Pamela's achievements and happy to resume their traditional role as grandparents. They stayed actively involved in their daughter and grandson's lives and were happy when Pamela met and married a man who became an excellent stepfather to Aaron.

This story offers some excellent guidelines for grandparents assuming custodial care of their grandchildren:

- *Put a child's safety first.* Aaron's behavior problems, a direct result of violence in the home, moved three caring adults to action. Pamela and her parents all put him first by moving the child to the calm and safety of the grandparents' home.
- *Agree on common goals.* Both the mother and grandparents intended for Aaron to be returned to Pamela's care. It's important to be clear on this issue, even if all parties agree to the initial custody arrangement. Through counseling, classes, and gradually increased visitation, movement toward reuniting parent and child should begin as quickly as possible.
- *Let the child get used to the new you.* Too often, a parent who "cleans up his act" expects a child's behavior to adjust immediately. This is unfair, to say the least. Trust and respect are earned, and it may take some time for once-neglectful parents to right the wrongs of their previous behavior and establish a healthy, positive relationship with their offspring.

Though in the case of Ann and Mike all parties were in agreement, custody and care issues can cause real problems within families, even when the parents have never abdicated their primary caregiver role. The following is a case in point.

Carlos and Theresa

Grief Divides a Family

When Carlos and Theresa met, Carlos had been widowed for three years after the death of his wife Celina from breast cancer. He was the father of two children. Theresa was the divorced mother of three.

In the years following Celina's death, Carlos relied heavily on her parents and siblings for help in rearing the children. Over these years, time did not bring the healing it usually does. Celina was revered in an almost saintly way, particularly by her immediate family. They clearly expected Carlos to remain single and work to preserve his wife's memory for all time. In later counseling, in fact, Carlos revealed that he felt Celina's family wanted him to become a "professional mourner."

At first this situation was fine for Carlos. He and Celina had been very happy together with a loving and stable marriage, and he certainly missed her. However, as time brought its natural healing, he realized that he needed and wanted to stop living in the past, and it was time for him and his children to move forward with life.

After a year and a half of focusing solely on his children, he decided he was ready to begin dating and develop an adult social life. After several months of meeting new people and dating casually, Carlos met Theresa, with whom he fell in love. This event did not thrill Celina's family, but they paid lip service to the fact that they were happy for him.

Carlos and Theresa married. As the children were quite young, the couple decided it would be best for Theresa to give up her part-time job and become a full-time caregiver, thereby offering the children increased continuity and security while eliminating some child-care expenses. Theresa and Carlos realized that this step could potentially create real problems, as Celina's family would have less responsibility for Carlos's children and probably perceive that change as another loss.

In an attempt to avoid this unhappy scenario, Theresa and Carlos took great care to involve the children in as many family activities as possible and to make sure that Celina's parents had an abundance of "grandparent time" with the children.

This was not enough for Celina's parents, who were quite young themselves. They began a rather insidious campaign to undermine Theresa in the eyes of their grandchildren. Carlos and Theresa quickly realized what was happening, but they continued to believe that time would heal everything. Unfortunately, that was not the case. Time brought about only greater animosity between the newly married couple and the grandparents.

Eventually Celina's parents lost all sense of perspective and began to twist what the children said until one day, in a desperate attempt to gain control over the children, they convinced themselves that Theresa was physically abusing the children. As a result of their wrongheaded conclusions, they filed a complaint with a local child protective agency, which conducted an investigation. The investigators concluded that not only was there no abuse by Theresa but that there was a concerted effort by Celina's parents to tear the young woman down in the eyes of her stepchildren.

As a result, a very angry Carlos and Theresa stopped all visitation between the children and grandparents. This situation was hard on the children, as they loved their grandparents and valued time with them, much of which was completely appropriate.

After much legal wrangling, the matter was brought to court. All parties involved were instructed to engage in the appropriate counseling, and a limited court-ordered schedule of supervised visitation with the grandparents began. Had therapeutic intervention been pursued earlier, it is more than likely that much of this extreme rancor could have been avoided.

This unfortunate scenario raises some interesting issues:

- *The grieving process is different for everyone.* There is nothing more personal than how an individual deals with loss, but, unfortunately, there is a tendency among people to judge others who don't grieve in the same way they do. Celina's parents expected Carlos's grief to evolve (or not) in exactly the way theirs had. When it didn't, trouble began.
- *Don't expect parents of a deceased spouse to be happy or accepting of a new relationship, at least not initially.* Although parents may intellectually understand their in-law's desire to move on, emotionally they may see it as a betrayal of their dead child.
- *Don't ignore danger signals.* Carlos and Theresa's combination of compassion and wishful thinking was disastrous. Given the time lapsed since Celina's death and her parents' devotion to her memory, it was unlikely that further passage of time would improve their feelings. The sooner an objective party intervenes, the better. Fortunately, the irrational behavior of Celina's parents didn't result in the removal of the children from Carlos's home. However, had the representative from social services been less insightful, a more undesirable outcome could have been possible.

As grandparents have become increasingly responsible for the care of their grandchildren, their push for court-recognized visitation and other rights has also increased. The last thing anyone wants or needs in an already traumatized family is a lengthy court battle. By addressing goals, respecting boundaries, and talking out difficulties sooner rather than later, parents and grandparents can work together to improve the lives of their children and extended families alike and offer everyone the opportunity to grow and move forward.

Sometimes, unfortunately, it is not possible for grandparents to step in to help care for the children when they must be removed from the home. In such cases, a temporary resolution of foster care or a permanent one of adoption is called for.

7

Blending Families Through Adoption and Foster Care

THE BIOLOGICAL AND social desire to procreate is a basic human goal. While some nations such as China and India are compelled to take government action to limit procreation, Americans have no such compulsion. The desire for children has led many couples to in vitro fertilization resulting in multiple births. For those who can't conceive or for whom a child need not be related by blood, the expansion of the family is achieved through adoption or foster parenting.

The U.S. Department of Health and Human Services data indicate that average life expectancy in 1990 was seventy-five years; in 1900 it was about forty-eight years. Individual life expectancy was once considerably less than it is today, and many hands were needed to help out on the farms, ranches, and plantations that were the primary means of family support. Thus, a large family was the norm. As the nation became more industrialized, women joined the workforce in increasing numbers and ultimately gained control over their ability to reproduce. As a result, families became smaller. The birthrate decreased and baby boomers typically had an average of one or two children. The large family appeared to be a thing of the past.

In recent years, that trend has again begun to reverse itself as more family blending is taking place. More and more couples are putting family ahead of work or finding ways to balance the two. More women are making compromises that make additions to the family possible. Couples who have delayed conception for the sake of their careers often require the assistance of fertility drugs and other reproductive procedures that inevitably result in multiple births. Meanwhile, there are those whose wish is simply to provide a home for a child who doesn't have one. These families have their lives enriched through the process of adoption.

Adoption

Adoption is the act of assuming permanent and complete legal rights to and responsibility for a child that is not biologically your own. The adoption process varies from state to state. Some states run adoption agencies directly from government offices; others license private agencies to arrange and implement adoptions. The process is often a lengthy one involving work with and the assessment of potential adoptive parents as well as the biological parent or parents preparing to part with their offspring. When the potential adoptee is old enough, he too is included in the preparations. Adoption can be an expensive undertaking, and those expenses are largely incurred by the parents-to-be. These expenses may include the medical and legal expenses of the birth mother, agency and attorney fees, and, in some circumstances, the living expenses of the birth mother for at least part of her pregnancy.

If the adoption is done via the foster care system, the steps involved are likely to be far more lengthy and complex. First, the biological parents may still have their parental rights, and those must be terminated before adoption can be accomplished. Even in instances of abuse or neglect, this is not a clear-cut process, as social service agencies have long favored family unification over termination. Many prospective parents' hearts have been broken when they have taken a child into their home under foster care and prepared to make him a permanent part of the family, only to have the biological parents fight and win for the right to keep the child. However, in recent years there has been a movement away from reunification at any cost, and limits are increasingly being set for how long a child can remain "in the system" before the parents stop receiving second chances and the child is free to move on with his life. That said, it's important for prospective adoptive parents to understand the possible risks, delays, and disappointments involved in such legal-risk adoption.

Another form of adoption is the private, or independent, adoption—a practice gaining in popularity. In these cases an intermediary, such as an attorney or a physician, can act to make a connection between birth parents and would-be adoptive parents. If you are considering this route, there are a couple of things to be cautious about. The first is expense. Make sure all these are deemed reasonable. The birth mother's legal and medical expenses should be taken care of, and many couples arrange for a stipend to ensure that she is comfortable and not overburdened by financial worries during the critical last month. This is not, however, an opportunity for the young woman to buy a car or pay off her college debts. In the most direct terms, there should be no exchange of monies that would even vaguely suggest that the child had been bought or sold.

Also, in many of these cases the adoption is not finalized until some months after the birth in order to ensure that the biological parents' rights have been fully honored and that no information has been concealed from them or undue pressure placed upon them.

While local adoption is often the easiest choice, it is certainly possible (and not uncommon) to adopt a child from another state or even another country. This is a more complicated and costly process and, in the case of the latter, one that involves the Immigration and Naturalization Service.

Parents, both birth and adoptive, must consider what adoption truly means. Traditionally, it meant the complete surrender of all ties and rights by the birth parents, and it unequivocally denied the rights of the child to uncover his biological history. Today, however, some states allow "open" adoptions by either mutual agreement of the adoptive and biological parents or the decree of the court. This means that some degree of visitation, or at the very least communication in the form of letters and pictures, is allowed between birth parent and child. This is most common when the child is older and has an established relationship with the birth parents or siblings with whom he wishes to maintain contact. There is, however, a small but growing movement of adoptive parents who include the birth parents in their child's life from the day they first bring the child home. In other states, open adoption is not allowed.

In addition to questions about how a child is adopted, there is the alternative question of who may adopt. Until recently, it was generally necessary to be part of a traditional married couple, one that could not conceive, in order to be considered as an adoptive parent. Today these criteria have changed, and there is significant flexibility afforded those who wish to be parents. Much more focus is now placed on the best interests of the child, as opposed to the marital status, religious affiliation, race, culture, or sexual orientation of the prospective parent or parents.

Even so, although single-parent adoptions have become quite common, both the states of Florida and New Hampshire continue to prohibit gay and lesbian adoptions. Florida's law has been declared unconstitutional, but that ruling is currently under appeal. Whether gay or straight, married or single, it's imperative to fully explore the different adoption laws in your state and county in order to have a successful and relatively stress-free adoption proceeding.

Although the focus of concern in adoption proceedings is generally the biological mother, the biological father also has rights and a role in the proceedings. Most states require that the biological father be notified if his child is to be placed for adoption. If he has a real interest in raising the child, he will generally be allowed to do so unless he is shown to be unfit. Fathers who do not wish to care for their children cannot force the biological mother to do so (the reverse is also true). Neither can they prohibit a woman from having an abortion, nor force her to do so. Legally, these decisions are the mother's right.

As mentioned previously, there was a time when those who wished to adopt but who already had their own biological children were automatically turned down. It was not considered a good idea to mix biological and adopted children within the same family. However, as time passed, the thinking on this issue changed. There are many good reasons why a couple or single parent might opt for adoption instead of having another biological child: a desire for a large family without multiple pregnancies, a need to give a child a home, a preference for an older child, and so on.

As wonderful as these thoughts and desires are, it is important to ask yourself some hard questions before embarking on the journey to adopt:

- Will you feel differently toward an adopted child than a biological child?
- Will an adopted child be "equal" with your biological children, and will the biological children accept the adopted child?
- Will your extended family accept the adopted child?
- Will an adopted child be viewed in any way as an outsider?
- Are you prepared to deal with any problems resulting from the child's previous environment?

The other thing to be prepared for when you adopt a child is that you may not immediately bond with him. Of course, the same may be true with biological children. Ask any parents with a number of children to tell the truth, and they'll admit that they bonded with some of their own children sooner than with others. For some adoptive parents there is an immediate attachment, a sense that the child was meant for them. For others, the same end result is achieved but only after some time.

How you handle the transition period—be it with an infant or a more mature child—will have an impact on not only your continuing relationship with that youngster but his relationships with siblings and extended family. Involving potential siblings in the planning process is important when considering adoption because the biological child needs to feel that his opinion is respected and valued within the family. Giving the child a sense of empowerment that comes from being a part of the process greatly improves the likelihood of a successful blending with the adopted sibling.

Parents should actively encourage and support a sense of connection among the new siblings. Pointing out common bonds, establishing new family traditions, as well as making sure special time is set aside for each of the children, not just the new arrival, all add to the development of a cohesive family unit.

One thing we have found to be true is that both adoptive and biological children need to parented with affection, concern, and reasonable and consistent limits. Focus should be on developmentally appropriate expectations and limits, not on whether or not the child is adopted. Children seem to put aside the issue of adoption rather easily and move on to the usual sibling conflicts such as space, pecking order, curfews, and the like.

Mitchell and Barbara

A Couple Who Blended Biological and Adoptive Children

Mitchell and Barbara already had a biological daughter, Emily, age eleven, when they decided to adopt seven-year-old Casey. The couple had always wanted a large family, but although Emily's conception and delivery were easy, Barbara was never able to get pregnant again. After some consideration they decided to adopt, as they didn't want Emily to grow up without a sibling. They wanted another daughter who would be old enough to begin immediately sharing experiences with Emily.

Both sets of grandparents had real concerns about this choice. They worried that a seven-year-old would be too set in her ways to blend in to the family and that additionally the child would likely have been through some difficult times that might make her behavior unmanageable. In fact, Casey had been born to a single mother with a history of drug abuse who was unable to care for her since infancy. Casey had been in two different foster homes, and both experiences were positive. The reason she had not previously been adopted was because parental rights were not terminated until she was nearly seven and her legal-risk status had scared away some prospective parents.

Emily was very involved in the process from the beginning and excited about the prospect of becoming a "big sister." Her parents assured her she played a vital role in the decision-making process. Emily and Casey got to know each other slowly, first with brief visits, then during overnight and week-end stays with the family. Casey had some ambivalence about leaving her foster family, of whom she'd grown quite fond, but they were experienced foster parents and helped Casey to move on, as they had with other children in the past. Fortunately for Casey, the family had always been clear with her that theirs was a foster, not a permanent, home, so she did not develop unrealistic expectations of that relationship.

Casey moved in to her adoptive home but continued to see her foster parents, albeit with less and less frequency. She was pleased to have become a permanent part of a family and took great pride in announcing "my family chose me."

In the years that followed, Mitchell and Barbara, like all parents, experienced some troubled times with the girls. Emily used the fact of Casey's adoption to torment her during fights. Casey rebelled against limits, particularly in her early adolescence, and justified the notion that she didn't need to follow rules by declaring she "wasn't really part of the family." The girls colluded to take money from the family "cookie jar," which was used for vacation savings, and instead used the funds to treat friends to candy. Mitchell and Barbara were often unsure whether the conflicts were typical or rooted in the fact of Casey's adoptive status. To help them sort it out, they maintained a long-term relationship with a therapist who had extensive experience with adoption issues. She was able to help the family sort out the root cause of various difficulties and deal with the reality that although Emily and Casey both felt the adoption was a blessing, it was also a weapon that they could use against one another in anger. Eventually the girls learned to accept and appreciate the permanence of family. One suggestion by the therapist was an annual Sister's Day celebration to honor the day that their sibling relationship became official. That celebration continues to this day, honoring the fact that though their family may be different, it is united in as enduring a manner as any other family.

Mitchell and Barbara's family makes no attempt to present their blended family in precisely the same way as a fully biological one, nor do they see it as a pale imitation of that traditional unit. Instead, it is appreciated for what it is—a blended family through adoption. This realistic stance has been very useful in normalizing the relationships among family members and has helped both girls to consolidate their respective identities.

We can take some lessons from this successful story of adoption:

- *If you already have biological children, involve them in the adoption process.* Because she was involved from the beginning, Emily never felt that her new sister was forced upon her.
- *Have a clear and realistic expectation of your expanded family.* Mitchell and Barbara gave a lot of thought to how the new arrival would affect their family, and they sought the assistance of a counselor to see them through the rough patches. By being proactive, they were immediately able to deal with problems and sort out what was typical sibling quarreling and what was unique to the adoption process.

Foster Parenting

Another way in which families can blend, albeit for a limited time, is through the foster parenting process. Since the 1950s, foster parenting has been the preferred and primary method of providing care to children who have been either temporarily or permanently removed from the care of their biological families. Rightfully it has been seen as a great improvement over the old orphanage system in which children were housed in institutional group settings. Currently the foster care system is undergoing something of a crisis, as the number of available foster families is decreasing while the number of needy children is on the rise.

According to the Child Welfare League, there are a number of reasons for the increased necessity for foster care in this country. Chief among the reasons are decreased support from mental health and juvenile justice systems that previously worked to help families stay together; increased assignments of children to protective care for problems of abuse and neglect; growing numbers of families dealing with issues of HIV/AIDS, chronic medical and physical handicaps, and substance abuse; and finally, increasingly lengthy stays by the children in foster homes.

Although it is a worthwhile and often rewarding role, not everyone is cut out to be a foster parent. Specifics vary from state to state, but there are some common guidelines for, and expectations of, those wishing to offer foster care. Prospective parents are screened and evaluated by professionals. They will undergo a background check for any criminal activity. They will attend training to become familiar with how to care for children who have significant medical or emotional needs. Physical and emotional characteristics of the home environment are evaluated. References are required and generally checked thoroughly. No one can become a foster parent without obtaining approval from an agency designed to assess and offer such certification, licensing, or acceptance.

While there are some core constraints, specific requirements do vary from agency to agency. Some require that the foster parent be economically self-sufficient and not desire certification merely for financial reasons. Some require a driver's license, others training in CPR and first aid. In other instances, a formal psychological screening is necessary. Suffice it to say, becoming a foster parent is an involved process, one that rightly places the potential caregivers under careful scrutiny. Once the parent is certified, there is generally a limit to the number of foster children that may reside in the foster home at any one time. Additionally, many foster families choose to specialize and so may deal primarily with a specific group such as younger children, medically at-risk or physically handicapped children, or children with learning disabilities.

Some states give foster parents the first option to adopt a child in their care after that child is freed from the legal ties to his biological parents. Other states prefer to view foster parents as professional, temporary resources. Whatever the state's view, many foster parents do end up adopting one or more of the children who have been placed in their care.

In recent years, legislation has moved toward not allowing children to languish in the foster care system for too long. This means that there are more clear-cut expectations of the biological parents and more focused attempts to provide the resources necessary for them to achieve those expectations. There are also time limits, as a growing consensus shows that allowing a child to remain in the uncertainty of the foster care system is inappropriate, damaging, and unfair to the child. No matter how much time or how many second chances the biological parent may request, the final decision about any termination of parental rights belongs to the court.

Another issue that has recently been addressed by legislation relates to the needs of young people who reach the age of eighteen while in the foster care system. At this age, many foster children have all support terminated. At a time when most children are going off to college with the loving support of their parents, these young people must suddenly find employment and lodging without any support system at all. To correct this frequently devastating situation, a bill named in honor of the late Senator John H. Chafee was signed into law in December 1999. The Care Independence Act and the John H. Chafee Foster Care Independence Program are aimed at helping those eighteen-year-olds who are exiting the foster care system obtain housing, education, vocational training, and health care. It recognizes the fact that an abrupt termination from the system can only be detrimental to those it was designed to assist.

Ultimately, the desire to love a child stretches across the boundaries of biology, race, religion, and culture. Most who adopt feel that although the child may not have been born of them, he was certainly meant for them. Loving foster parents, even those who have the care of a child briefly, can offer a vision of themselves that may make the difference between a child who contributes to society or one who drops out of it. The world may see these parents as noble, but most foster parents will tell you that they feel that the greatest beneficiaries of the decision to open up their home and their lives to a child was themselves.

8

Blending Adults into Existing Families

THROUGHOUT THIS BOOK we have explored the most commonly acknowledged changes of a family structure: divorce, remarriage, and the addition of children. There are, however, other ways in which a family can be altered, and many of these involve the addition of an extra adult into the household. Many families now find themselves becoming part of what is popularly referred to as the "sandwich generation," squeezed between the needs of young children and aging parents, both of whom require their time and care. In other cases, older adults, ready to be alone with their mate after their childrearing years, find themselves confronted with an adult child who, for any variety of reasons, wants to live with them once again. Finally, when a working couple needs additional assistance, a full-time nanny may be brought into the home to ensure the children have regular and consistent oversight. Or couples may hire a nurse or caretaker to aid with an ailing parent in the home. This chapter will examine each of these situations and their implications.

In an ideal world, no good person would ever feel that he or she was forced to make a choice between caring for a parent and caring for a child. Yet today, many are faced with just such a dilemma. A number of factors contribute to this. First and foremost, people in general—

by virtue of better living conditions and medical advances—are living longer. Longevity, unfortunately, does not often contribute to quality of life. In fact, poor health and economic hardship are not at all uncommon among the elderly. Many are frequently forced to choose between decent food and appropriate medication.

While there has been a tremendous growth in assisted-living facilities, some financial backing is required to even consider this option; in truth, it is truly viable only for middle- to upper-middle-income families. It is certainly not an option for those with very limited funds or who are dependent upon Social Security. Therefore, a segment of the elderly population must depend rather heavily upon their families for care and support.

The other half of this "sandwich" is much younger and made up of adult children who, due to the vagaries of the workplace and need for specialized skills in order to make a living wage in our technology-driven economy, frequently and perhaps suddenly find themselves out of work. The days of being employed by a company and becoming part of a workplace "family" are long gone. In past generations, it was typical to work for one company for an entire career, but that is certainly not the case today. Even those who are highly trained, well educated, and ambitious find themselves unemployed as a result of corporate takeovers, downsizing, and folding start-up companies. As a result, many return to the family home on a temporary basis while seeking new employment or while receiving new or additional training to make themselves more appealing to employers.

Marlene

A "Sandwich" Caretaker's Dilemma

Marlene was a fifty-four-year-old married woman with two grown children, Allan and Phillip. Allan, twenty-three, was in graduate school; Phillip, twenty-seven, had recently moved back home, as he was between jobs and experiencing financial difficulties. Marlene could deal with Phillip's return, but the timing was complicated by the fact that, simultaneously, her eighty-year-old mother, Grace, had begun to decline physically and emotionally.

Marlene and Grace's relationship had always been somewhat strained, as Grace was often self-centered and generally preoccupied with her own needs. She also complained a great deal and approached life with a negative attitude. Nevertheless, the passing of her second husband left Grace financially secure, and she was able to purchase a home in Florida as well as maintain the family residence approximately an hour and a half from Marlene's home.

The family became aware of the fact that Grace's health was slipping, and her decline was quite rapid. Her deterioration created a great deal of stress among the immediate family. Marlene's brother, Stanley, felt that their mother should move in with Marlene and then spend some time with him and his family, but they resided in another state. Stanley's second wife, Brenda, had two children of her own. When Grace stayed at their home, it was apparent that Brenda, not Stanley, looked after her needs during those visits.

The children ultimately realized that Grace's needs would be best met if she did not have to move back and forth between Marlene and Stanley. An immediate alternative was to place Grace in an assisted-living environment. However, the decision had to be made as to whether that residence would be close to Marlene or to Stanley. This decision-making process resulted in additional stress for all involved while they attempted to discern what Grace really wanted and could accept. Both of her children had feelings of ambivalence and guilt about placing her in a situation that would rob her of the independence that she had previously enjoyed.

Meanwhile, Stanley was pressuring Marlene to become her mother's primary caretaker. Marlene's son Phillip strongly objected to this scenario and said that if Grandma Grace moved in, he'd be moving out, complaining that "She's doom and gloom and makes everyone around her depressed."

Marlene's husband, who previously had stayed out of the fray, now rallied to Marlene's aid and became a great personal support system for her. With his encouragement she sought professional help to try and sort out the housing issues as well as deal with her own emergent anxiety and depression. Through short-term counseling, Marlene was able to examine her relationship with her mother and make practical and objective decisions regarding what would be in everyone's best interest while reducing her level of stress. She also began to understand how to be more appropriately assertive with both her mother and her brother.

As a result, Stanley was forced to accept that his mother needed to be placed in an assisted-living situation. Grace was financially capable of taking care of such an arrangement, and although Stanley's inheritance would decrease, his sister's sanity would remain intact. Further and quite vocal support for this arrangement was offered by Stanley's wife, Brenda.

The final result was that Grace moved into an assisted-living situation near Marlene, who was able to look after her consistently and spend limited but quality time with her on holidays and weekends while still enjoying her husband and children. Ultimately this was a good decision for all.

Lessons to be learned from Marlene:

- *Don't let others make your decisions for you.*
  Certainly it was in Stanley's best interest for Marlene to become their mother's primary caregiver; he knew their mother would receive excellent care and could absolve himself of any guilt about her daily life. However, what was good for Stanley was totally unfair to Marlene. Understanding that others can be entirely self-serving in their suggestions can keep you from making potentially disastrous decisions.
- *Be realistic.* Know what you are and are not capable of as a caretaker, and act accordingly.

While separate living situations were best in Marlene's case, there are situations in which an elderly relative can move in with a family to everyone's benefit. A good example of this is the story of Sam.

Sam

When an Aging Parent Can't Live Alone

Sam was an eighty-five-year-old widower and father of three daughters. His health was failing physically but not mentally, and he was loath to admit he needed assistance, as he had always led an independent lifestyle. Sam had never left his childhood neighborhood. He played golf and spent time with his cronies with whom his connections were strong after eighty-five years. But as time passed, the physical problems of aging affected them all.

Sam had established a small manufacturing business, and it continued under the oversight of his eldest daughter's husband. Sam still served as a consultant to the business and enjoyed a close relationship with his son-in-law and daughters. The other two girls were unmarried; one lived in Europe, where she worked as a translator for a fashion house; the other was a professional who worked in a metropolitan area not far from Sam's suburban neighborhood. While close to her father, this daughter was frequently away from home, as the responsibilities of her job involved long hours and travel. Because of their career circumstances, neither of these siblings was well suited to become Sam's caretaker.

Fortunately, all the girls enjoyed a good relationship, both with their father and with each other. They were able to talk openly about their father's situation and together plan how they might best care for him. After discussing various options, they met with Sam and suggested to him that he should move in with his eldest daughter and her husband. After a brief initial period of hesitancy, Sam agreed to the plan and made the move. As a result, he was able to keep abreast of both the goings-on at his company and activities of his immediate family.

Although Sam was not able to spend as much time as he used to with neighborhood friends, he saw family members on a more regular basis and, as a result, became far better acquainted with the younger generation. The whole family agreed that this served to enhance his life and keep his spirits up. Sam's grandchildren, in particular, were very happy about his increased involvement in their lives, as his consistent presence enabled them to learn a great deal about their family history and particularly about the grandmother they'd never had a chance to meet.

Lessons to be learned from Sam's situation:

- *When making a commitment to take in an elderly parent, it is important to be clear on what the responsibilities involved will be.* Although nothing is certain in life, you can assess potential situations based on the personality of the parent and the nature of your relationship with him or her.
- *If you have children living with you, it is important to consider how this decision will affect them.* For Sam's grandchildren it was clearly an enriching experience, but each family must honestly and objectively evaluate the truth of its own situation.
- *Realize what you are capable of.* For example, if the parent who is moving in with you had an active social life prior to the move, it will be necessary to help maintain those relationships and activities that greatly contribute to his or her physical and mental well-being.
- *Finally, make sure that this new responsibility does not take control of your own life.* Remember that as a caretaker you have new responsibilities, but you

are also entitled to continue to do the things that are important and enriching for you personally. For this reason it's vital to have alternative care providers who can step in as necessary to provide you with some time off.

Louis and Esther

Children Supportive of Their Aging Parents

Older people frequently form romantic companionship relationships with individuals whom they don't marry. The reasons for not formalizing these unions are conscious decisions generally revolving around finances. In some cases, benefits may be threatened by marriage; in others, the mixing of assets that will be handed down to children and grandchildren is simply not desired. Regardless of marital status, these individuals become part of their mate's larger extended family and can affect—for better or worse—their relationships with those family members.

Louis and Esther met while wintering in Florida after both had lost their spouses. Louis, eighty-one when they met, and Esther, fifteen years his junior, happily discovered that in addition to the proximity of their winter homes in Florida, they each had homes in the same Massachusetts community. The relationship evolved over time, and the couple eventually decided that Esther would share Louis's Florida home with him, though they continued to maintain separate residences in Massachusetts.

Although there were some stresses, as there are in any relationship, the two were quite compatible, and their children were supportive of their relationship. Over time, Louis's health began to diminish, and his dependence on Esther increased. It became more and more unfair to burden Esther with the role of primary caretaker for Louis. His needs were extensive, and the family became concerned for his safety while he was staying with Esther. Although Esther was supportive and wanted to do all she could, she objectively listened to the concerns of Louis's family and understood that his needs for care were surpassing her capacity to provide them. Because this situation was fraught with potential for hurt feelings and miscommunication, the support of Esther's and Louis's families was crucial.

It was decided that Louis would best be served by moving into an assisted-living environment. As is the case with most people who reach this stage, Louis did not greet the prospect of losing some of his independence enthusiastically. However, the transition took place with the support, understanding, and reassurance of all involved. Esther was given Louis's Florida home by his children as an expression of their appreciation for the many positive contributions she had made to his life.

Esther maintained contact with Louis and visited him periodically. Happily, she went on to develop a new relationship, which she shared with Louis's supportive children but kept from Louis so he wouldn't be hurt.

Lessons to be learned from Louis and Esther:

- *Respect your parent's partner, even if they haven't made it legal.* Louis's family showed Esther respect and appreciation; consequently, she was able to see the wisdom of no longer living with the man she'd loved for 15 years. Taking a dismissive or proprietary attitude in such situations can cause real turmoil and often have seriously adverse effects on the health of one or both members of the elderly couple.
- *If you've lost one parent, encourage and support the other to get on with life.* Too often children see their parent's new relationship as a threat or disrespectful to the memory of the departed mother or father. This

is unfortunate because life is truly for the living. There are many benefits to the children if the aging parent has someone to share his or her life with.

Caretakers in the Home

Another way adults move into families is by becoming caregivers, and one of the more delicate relationships is with the nannies of young children. Historically the nanny was a family retainer who joined the household and stayed for many years, often helping to raise several generations or at the least seeing children through their teenage years.

Nowadays, nannies or au pairs may join a family and remain for a year, only to be replaced by another the following year. These people, generally young women, often come from foreign countries or different cultures. Their role in the family varies from family to family. In some there are clear boundaries between the nanny and the parents; in others nannies become almost a member of the family. When the latter is the case, it can greatly complicate their departure, when it becomes necessary, and have a significant emotional impact upon the children involved. In many instances, these professional parent surrogates have a greater influence on the child's daily life than the biological parents do. Like most relationships, this situation can be simple, or it can be complicated. An excellent example of how this scenario can become quite complex is the story of Adam.

Adam

A Case of Too Many Caregivers

Adam was eight years old; his parents divorced when he was four. Both parents were well-to-do professionals who arranged for joint custody. Because of the time involved in pursuing their careers, each enlisted the services of a nanny. Needless to say, this was a relatively pressure-free position for each young woman, as each had the care of the child for only half of each week. Within two years of the divorce, each parent remarried, and Adam's stepmother also had a child, two years older than Adam.

In the case of Adam's mother, the nanny would change each year; the nanny hired by his father had been with him since the beginning and became a significant adult in Adam's life. Adam was clearly attached to her, and this closeness led to some conflicts in his relationship with his stepmother. This problem occurred despite the fact that both stepmother and nanny had worked hard to encourage the development of a good stepparent-child relationship. However, the nanny's presence in the household was vital because, as in the previous marriage, both partners were busy professionals.

A different set of problems existed with the nannies at his mother's house. Because none of these caregivers stayed longer than a year, Adam quickly determined not to form a strong connection to them. As a result, his relationships with these caregivers were far more conflict ridden. Adam regularly tended to manipulate them, far different behavior from what he exhibited with his longtime nanny at his father's house.

This striking difference in behavior caused both sets of parents to seek professional help. Adam needed a neutral place to express his feelings about not only his new stepfamilies but the nannies as well. After speaking with Adam, the therapist decided to meet with both sets of parents, where it was established that Adam's new sibling was also having trouble adjusting.

As a result, Adam's stepmother decided to begin working from home part-time so that she could be more involved in the children's daily lives. His father and stepmother also decided to engage a caregiver who would have far less responsibility for the children, primarily looking after them in the afternoon during the hours between when school let out and the time the parents returned home.

Interestingly, the long-term nanny, who regularly felt caught in the middle, was pleased with this new arrangement and quickly found another full-time position. Her acceptance of this situation went a long way toward easing the transition and relieving feelings of guilt experienced by Adam's father.

As the parents continued to work with the therapist, it was agreed that Adam's needs would best be met by increasing the time spent with his father and stepmother. This couple was able to offer more consistent personal time to him than could his mother, whose work schedule was increasingly demanding and involved quite a bit of travel. The change in arrangements meant that Adam spent the week with his father and three-day weekends with his mother. This schedule gave each set of parents quality time with Adam as well as the flexibility to pursue their careers.

What made the resolution of this complex scenario possible was his parents' ability to behave logically and remain focused on Adam's best interests. Parents may well believe that offering a variety of involved adults in the form of caregivers is in the child's best interests, but often, as in this case, the opposite is true. Too many cooks were spoiling the soup, namely the security and consistency a child needs for happy and positive development.

Lessons to be learned from Adam's situation:

- *Children suffer from divided loyalties.* In this case, there were simply too many caretakers in Adam's life, and he was more attached to some than others. This created real conflict for the boy, which was apparent when he acted out. Try not to put children in a situation where they may have to choose between loved ones. It's very distressing for them.

- *Prioritize*. Parents can't have it all, and trying to can cause real hardships for the kids. With compromise, however, there's no reason you cannot pursue work you love and love your child. You may simply need to adjust your vision of success and trade in that second promotion for a front-row seat at the second-grade holiday pageant.

Amanda

Consistency Is Key in Caregiving

Amanda was the only child born to a physician-attorney couple who divorced when she was five. Each wished to have a hands-on role in raising their daughter, and each certainly respected the role of the other parent. However, neither parent could guarantee any consistent personal time. Consequently, they agreed to share a nanny and have her move from home to home rather than utilize multiple caretakers.

This situation had the additional benefit of providing each parent a set of eyes and ears that could help them keep their parenting styles as consistent as possible. It minimized Amanda's ability to manipulate her parents and play upon the guilt they felt for time spent away from her. Over time, as Amanda grew older and more independent and involved in school activities, the need for the nanny gradually decreased until Amanda turned twelve, at which point the nanny's services were no longer necessary.

Lessons to be learned from Amanda's situation:

- *Work with your ex-spouse as much as possible*. It can't be said often enough: putting aside your conflicts as a couple in order to look after the best interests of the child is the difference between a happy child and a troubled one.

- *Children thrive with consistency.* Having the same caretaker gave Amanda a multitude of benefits: a positive attachment to a loving caregiver, diminished opportunity for manipulation and acting out, and the safety of knowing that her parents, though separated, were working together.

As the previous examples illustrate, changes in the modern American lifestyle have had a significant impact upon the ways our families need to readjust. The fastest growing segment of our population is the eighty-five and older age group. Of this population, approximately 58 percent are disabled in some way. Therefore, helpers such as nursing assistants, visiting nurses, and various types of allied health professionals become, at least for a while, temporary members of the family.

Systems that provide such support have not kept up with demand. Those who take these jobs rarely see them as long-term positions; for most, they are merely stepping-stones to further education and professional status. As a result, turnover is high in these jobs, and many elderly people find that they have adjusted to one home health care worker only to discover that another has taken his or her place. The majority filling these jobs are women; in fact, 80 percent of those caring for both children and the elderly are female. These caregivers receive little in the way of institutional support, and those who do their best ultimately realize that they need to look after their own needs as well as the needs of others.

When dealing with the care of the elderly and/or infirm, it is important to set realistic goals, understand what the family is able to offer, and know when to seek professional help. Gone are the days when extended families lived in close proximity and older female family members were available to help young mothers, or when younger women stayed at home with children and could also assist elderly relatives by running errands or cooking meals. This family dynamic has altered to the point that only the rarest of households do not or will not need the support of an unrelated adult caregiver. It's important to accept this reality rather than force yourself or your family to live up to some unrealistic Norman Rockwell standard of behavior. The fact is, we all have our limits—of time, patience, stamina, and knowledge; working within those limits will greatly enhance the prospect of a satisfying extended family life.

Although the caregiver issue generally affects the middle-aged most significantly, it also has an impact on younger families. This is especially true of those whose children suffer from chronic illness or developmental disabilities for which they require specialized care. Fortunately, the trend has moved away from institutionalizing such children. Even though interaction in the community benefits not just disabled children but everyone around them, there is an unfortunate shortage of readily available support, and many of those who could certainly benefit from outside assistance are unable to receive it.

Some of the services that enable families to keep disabled parents or children at home as viable members of the family unit include adult day-care services and respite-care services. Other organizations can even provide such services as supervised vacations for the handicapped, who would otherwise not be able to travel safely.

Marion and Joyce

A Painful but Positive Plan

Marion was the elderly mother of Joyce, a daughter with Down syndrome, now in middle age. For years Marion and her husband provided all of Joyce's care, supported only by several evening programs for socialization. When Joyce's father passed away, Marion found herself alone in caring for her daughter. Although Joyce had been taught many basic daily living skills and spent her days in a sheltered environment, Marion became increasingly concerned about what would happen to Joyce, an only child, when she was no longer able to care for her. Her biggest fear was that Joyce would have to adjust to both the death of her mother and a new living situation at the same time.

With the help of local and state associations for retarded citizens, Marion was able to band together with other parents in the same predicament and develop a living environment for Joyce and four other women with similar issues. Although Marion was sad to see Joyce move out, she was pleased to have some control over the site selection and hiring of staff for her daughter's residence. She helped Joyce make the transition while enjoying frequent contact with her daughter. Joyce's adjustment took several months. But with the help of support staff and professionals, this difficult task was successfully implemented.

As with any situation, those who are the most informed, persistent, and vocal in their quest for service are the most likely to receive assistance with a disabled family member. It is best and generally correct to assume, particularly when dealing with a government agency, that those in charge are overburdened with both clients and caseloads. To successfully navigate this troubled bureaucracy, we offer the following tips:

- *Arrange a face-to-face meeting with anyone responsible for providing or issuing the provision of services to you or a family member.* As a result, you become a person, not just another voice on the phone or letter in the mailbox.
- *Keep a paper trail and document all plans, time lines, and so on.* Most service providers genuinely wish to help others, but that doesn't negate the fact that they are usually overworked. Good documentation can make all the difference when things fall through the cracks.
- *Try to connect with service providers at times other than those when you're making demands upon them.* Drop a note to let them know you appreciate them, drop some cookies by

the office—anything that recognizes the good they do. We all know from our own experience that few things motivate like appreciation.

- *Before you contact a service provider, do your homework.* When you do contact them, be able to clearly and succinctly articulate your needs. If the provider you've contacted isn't able to assist you, don't hesitate to request a referral to one who can.

- *Be a joiner.* Even if your schedule doesn't allow for regular participation in a group that addresses your needs, join anyway and read the newsletter while participating when you can. Information is power.

- *Follow legislation that relates to your situation, and make contact with your legislators when possible.* Whether as an advocate or registered voter, make your concerns known to your elected officials.

- *Don't be afraid to seek professional guidance if you're feeling overwhelmed by family responsibilities.* Sometimes all you need is to be able to blow off steam in order to muster your resources and move on to the next challenge.

- *Consider developing relationships with others in the same position.* Sharing mutual frustrations and practical solutions can offer a breadth of understanding and resources you might not have imagined.

The trend toward dealing with dependent children and aging parents is a modern fact of life. Accurately assess your capacities, flexibility, and priorities, or you run the risk of becoming a martyr and burning out in the process. Engage not only in the care of needy family members but in your own care as well. Learning to reach out and let others help may be the greatest lesson of all.

Appendix

Guidelines for a Successful Blended Family

THE FOLLOWING PRACTICAL guidelines will help remind you of many of the common problems faced by blending families so that you can address them in a proactive manner. If you are planning to engage a therapist to help with the blending process, these lists may help you to focus on the issues that are affecting you most and help you use your time in counseling in the most effective way possible.

Finding a Therapist

Before we get to specifics of blending families, let us first address the issue of finding a therapist. As in any profession, there are good ones and bad ones. From among the many good ones, however, a family must ascertain which professional is right for them.

When looking for a therapist, the first thing we suggest is don't look in the Yellow Pages! Almost anyone can advertise and represent him- or herself as a therapist. A much better place to begin is with your primary care physician. In all likelihood, he or she has an established relationship and strong professional alliance with a variety of such professionals. Knowing both you and your potential therapist means that your physician is in a good position to help you make the right match. A proper fit is very important in a psychotherapeutic relation-ship—perhaps more important than it is in any other type of health care relationship.

Not everyone has a primary care physician, or they may have one who does not have a reference list of recommended therapists. In that case, you can refer to professional organizations of mental health pro-fessionals (see Resources). Although not all licensed mental health professionals belong to such organizations, these organizations can be the first step in finding and evaluating the right therapist for you. Every state has a psychological association, including one for social workers and family and marriage counselors. Often, these associations are located at the state capital. They maintain referral services that identify professionals by specialty, area of expertise, and geographic location.

When considering professional support, look for appropriate licen-sure. Although being licensed is certainly no guarantee that a therapist is right for you, it does provide a standard that assures you the clini-cian you're considering has mastered a certain body of relevant knowl-edge and has worked under the supervision of an experienced clinician of the same discipline. It should be noted that there are some talented clinicians who follow a more nontraditional path. However, lacking a baseline standard for judging such alternative practices makes it diffi-cult to discern who among them might provide good care. It should also be noted that health insurance companies do not reimburse for care that is not provided by appropriately licensed agencies or indi-viduals. Financial considerations play a major role in almost any fam-ily decision, and therapy is no exception. Additionally, most health management organizations (HMOs) have their own restricted list of practitioners whose services are reimbursable under your contract with them. Therefore, always check with your insurance carrier to maxi-mize your coverage and avoid an unhappy surprise when the therapist's bill arrives.

Another good source when seeking a therapist trained in dealing with blending issues is a matrimonial lawyer. If you are blending as a result of divorce, your attorney is probably in a good position to make some recommendations regarding clinicians trained and experienced in this arena.

Once you have made an initial determination as to which therapist might be right for you, the next important step is to schedule a face-to-face meeting. Take the time to assess whether you and the therapist are suited. Gut reactions are important at this stage. Regardless of training or reputation, no single individual is equipped to deal well with everyone.

Now that we've established how to find a therapist, we will go through the guidelines we hope will proactively help in your quest for a successfully blended family.

Coping with Divorce

When the decision to split is finally made, the participants are generally overwhelmed by a sense of hurt, anger, and betrayal. Focus on what's important.

- *Remember the children, the children, and the children.* Whenever anger, fear, or depression overcome you, you can't go wrong by putting your children's needs before your own unhappiness. If you feel the urge to spend a few hours at your attorney's office arguing over who gets grandma's silver, imagine how much better that time and money might be spent—at Disneyland, perhaps!
- *Cut your losses.* So often people dwell on the time spent with their spouse as if it was lost or wasted because of the divorce. Of course that isn't true. Good memories, life lessons, and, most important, beautiful children have been the result of the union. The only time wasted is that spent dwelling on the past when you could be moving on toward the future.
- *Take care of the practicalities.* This is not a time to be stupid or noble. An equitable division of assets is necessary on a practical and emotional level. Not only are there children to look after, but there's no reason one partner should exit a long-term marriage either far better or worse off than the other. This is where the "equitable" part kicks in. Engaging in a long-term financial battle with a spouse as a way of

getting back at him or her enriches only the attorneys. Worse, it robs you of things you can never get back: time, happiness, and dignity.

- *Seek help.* There are going to be days when you might need a good cry or one too many beers in the company of friends. This is when your friends are happy to step up and take the kids, or you, for the night. Not only does nobody expect you to be perfect, they'll be relieved that you're not.

- *Use extended family as a support mechanism, not a weapon.* Unless there is some threat posed by your former spouse, don't insist that your family turn against him or her. Certainly you won't all be having Sunday brunches together, but they will likely come in contact, particularly if you share children or live in a small community. It's wrong to make people choose sides or deny an affection that may have developed for a person over the years. Certainly establish boundaries for discussing your former spouse or dismissing any misguided attempt at orchestrating a reunion between the two of you. Be the bigger person and move on.

- *Talk to your kids.* This doesn't mean putting them in the role of best friend; don't use them as a sounding board for complaints about your ex. Do, however, be willing to share that you are also sad and scared, and let them know that they have a perfect right to all of their feelings, although they do not have a right to act upon them in any way they'd like.

Preparing to Blend a Family

Once you are ready to move on, there is a whole new set of challenges to be met. The following list covers the basics that a family preparing to blend must consider.

- *Clarity and commonality of goals for the relationship.* Simply stated, are you sure that you know what you're getting into? Have you analyzed the risk factors? Are your expectations clear? Do they match the expectations of your proposed partner? Most important, are your shared expectations realistic given your particular situation?

If you are unsure about any of these answers, it is best to proceed with caution and seek advice from an appropriately trained counselor. The advice of family and friends is generally sincere, but it may not be objective. If real questions exist, it is best to explore them with a professional. Many a friendship or family has been damaged because well-intended but inappropriate advice was given.

- *Willingness to adapt.* If you have completed the first step in this process, it is now time to assess the issue of compromise. Explore whether or not you are willing and able to make the changes necessary in your lifestyle to accommodate a reasonable outcome. Have candid conversations with your proposed partner and any other involved parties about what the compromises might be and who will make them.

- *Motivation for the relationship/blend.* At this point you have clarified a great deal about your impending commitment. Examine motivational factors and assure yourself that you are not entering this relationship to escape from a previously painful one. Now is the time to assure yourself that you are entering your new relationship with a sense of flexibility and reality rather than a fantasized notion of what lies ahead.

- *Authority.* It is important to work together to establish a plan so that the new parent neither over- nor underexpresses his or her authority. Initially at least it is best if the stepparent functions as a monitor of the stepchild's behavior, taking on more the posture of an additional caregiver rather than the ultimate parental authority figure.

- *Family and career.* Through separation, divorce, and remarriage all participants must devise a plan of action with which to balance schedules, career, and family. The sooner this is addressed, the better.

- *Housing.* Particularly in those cases where one family is moving into what has long been the primary residence of the other, make sure you find a way to reflect, as much as possible, the new family unit while respecting the long-established boundaries of the old one.

- *Bonding.* Once remarriage takes place, everyone must be prepared for and adjust to the fact that there will be a reduction in the one-on-one time spent between noncustodial parent and child. Although it is clear that bonding between stepparents and children is important to the child's well-being, a real dilemma can occur if this bonding process diminishes the bond between the child and his or her biological parent.
- *The divorce chain.* This dilemma refers to the decision-making process about who is and isn't really a part of the new family. Questions that may arise include such issues as whether or not nonresidential children are part of the household.

The Final Blending

Every process has a final stage. This involves the normalization of all that has been worked on up to this point. It is the time in which things begin to become more automatic and a higher degree of interpersonal trust and emotional closeness has developed among family members.

It is clear that, like many processes in life, there is a pattern to this final stage. Nonetheless, these things take time, and many factors can intervene. Thus, patience is essential. The process of blending a family is not easy and rarely occurs without real setbacks.

Following are some basic guidelines that will help the ever-increasing number of people involved in this process to move forward:

- *Make sure that you have examined and understand the basic issues that resulted in the dissolution of your previous partnership.*
- *Make sure that you and your new partner are clear with one another on the basic vision you share for your newly created family.*
- *Take time to assess any hidden anger, jealousy, or mistrust that might interfere with the process.*

- *Be honest about the real role you might play in any difficulty.* It is all too easy to blame problems on others.
- *Understand that your children are people, too, and that their thoughts and feelings need to be respected.* Do not assume that they will automatically be ready to embrace your view of things.
- *Respect your former spouse's views when it comes to parenting.*
- *Do not be afraid to seek professional help if you get stuck.* It is not a sign of weakness or failure. Remember, in order to complete any important project successfully, at times we need to go out and buy tools we don't currently possess.

There is no blueprint for success, but it is our hope that these guidelines will help you navigate the difficult but rewarding process of blending a family.

Resources

To Find Licensed or Certified Therapists

Alabama

Alabama Psychological Association
P.O. Box 97
Montgomery, AL 36101-0097
(314) 262-8245

National Association of Social Workers: Alabama Chapter
2921 Marti Lane, #G
Montgomery, AL 36116
(334) 288-2633

Alaska

Alaska Psychological Association
P.O. Box 241292
Anchorage, AK 99524-1292
(907) 344-8878

National Association of Social Workers: Alaska Chapter
4220 Resurrection Drive
Anchorage, AK 99504
(907) 332-6279

Arizona

Arizona Psychological Association
6210 E. Thomas Road, Suite 209
Scottsdale, AZ 85251
(480) 675-9477

National Association of Social Workers: Arizona Chapter
610 West Broadway, #116
Tempe, AZ 85282
(480) 968-4595

Arkansas

Arkansas Psychological Association
1123 South University, Suite 235
Little Rock, AR 72204
(501) 614-6500

National Association of Social Workers: Arkansas Chapter
1123 South University, Suite 1010
Little Rock, AR 72204
(501) 663-0658

California

California Psychological Association
1022 G Street
Sacramento, CA 95814-0817
(916) 325-9786

National Association of Social Workers: California Chapter
1016 Twenty-third Street
Sacramento, CA 95816
(916) 442-4565

Colorado

Colorado Psychological Association
1660 South Albion, Suite 712
Denver, CO 80222
(303) 692-9303

National Association of Social Workers: Colorado Chapter
6000 East Evans, Building 1, Suite 121
Denver, CO 80222
(303) 753-8890

Connecticut

Connecticut Psychological Association
342 North Main Street
West Hartford, CT 06117-2507
(860) 586-7522

National Association of Social Workers: Connecticut Chapter
2139 Silas Deane Highway, Suite 205
Rocky Hill, CT 06067
(860) 257-8066

Delaware

Delaware Psychological Association
P.O. Box 718
Claymont, DE 19703-0718
(302) 478-2591

National Association of Social Workers: Delaware Chapter
3301 Green Street
Claymont, DE 19703
(302) 792-0646

District of Columbia

District of Columbia Psychological Association
750 First Street NE, Suite 7306
Washington, DC 20002-4241
(202) 336-5559

National Association of Social Workers: DC Metro Chapter
P.O. Box 75236
Washington, DC 20013
(202) 371-8282

Florida

Florida Psychological Association
408 Office Plaza
Tallahassee, FL 32301-2757
(850) 656-2222

National Association of Social Workers: Florida Chapter
345 South Magnolia Drive, Suite 14-B
Tallahassee, FL 32301
(850) 224-2400

Georgia

Georgia Psychological Association
1750 Century Circle, Suite 10
Atlanta, GA 30345
(404) 634-6272

National Association of Social Workers: Georgia Chapter
3070 Presidential Drive, Suite 226
Atlanta, GA 30340
(770) 234-0567

Hawaii

Hawaii Psychological Association
P.O. Box 10456
Honolulu, HI 96816-0456
(808) 521-8995

National Association of Social Workers: Hawaii Chapter
680 Iwilei Road, Suite 665
Honolulu, HI 96817
(808) 521-1787

Idaho

Idaho Psychological Association
P.O. Box 352
Boise, ID 83701-0352
(208) 375-0125

National Association of Social Workers: Idaho Chapter
P.O. Box 7393
Boise, ID 83707
(208) 343-2752

Illinois

Illinois Psychological Association
203 North Wabash, #1404
Chicago, IL 60601-2413
(312) 372-7610

National Association of Social Workers: Illinois Chapter
180 North Michigan Avenue, Suite 400
Chicago, IL 60601
(312) 236-8308

Indiana

Indiana Psychological Association
55 Monument Circle, Suite 455
Indianapolis, IN 46204
(317) 686-5348

National Association of Social Workers: Indiana Chapter
1100 West Forty-second Street, Suite 375
Indianapolis, IN 46208
(317) 923-9878

Iowa

Iowa Psychological Association
P.O. Box 320
Knoxville, IA 50138-0320
(515) 828-8845

National Association of Social Workers: Iowa Chapter
4211 Grand Avenue, Level 3
Des Moines, IA 50312
(515) 277-1117

Kansas

Kansas Psychological Association
901B Southwest Tenth
Topeka, KS 66604
(785) 354-8430

National Association of Social Workers: Kansas Chapter
Jayhawk Towers
700 Southwest Jackson Street, Suite 801
Topeka, KS 66603-3740
(785) 354-4804

Kentucky

Kentucky Psychological Association
120 Sears Avenue, Suite 202
Louisville, KY 40207-5014
(502) 894-0777

National Association of Social Workers: Kentucky Chapter
310 St. Clair Street, Suite 104
Frankfort, KY 40601
(270) 223-0245

Louisiana

Louisiana Psychological Association
P.O. Box 66924
Baton Rouge, LA 70896-6924
(225) 344-8839

National Association of Social Workers: Louisiana Chapter
700 North Tenth Street, Suite 200
Baton Rouge, LA 70802
(225) 346-5035

Maine

Maine Psychological Association
P.O. Box 5435
Augusta, ME 04330
(800) 287-5065

National Association of Social Workers: Maine Chapter
222 Water Street
Hallowell, ME 04347
(207) 622-7592

Maryland

Maryland Psychological Association
1 Mall North, Suite 314
10025 Governor Warfield Parkway
Columbia, MD 21044
(410) 992-4258
(301) 596-3999

National Association of Social Workers: Maryland Chapter
5710 Executive Drive, Suite 105
Baltimore, MD 21228
(410) 788-1066

Massachusetts

Massachusetts Psychological Association
14 Beacon Street, #714
Boston, MA 02108-3741
(617) 263-0080

National Association of Social Workers: Massachusetts Chapter
14 Beacon Street, Suite 409
Boston, MA 02108-3741
(617) 227-9635

Michigan

Michigan Psychological Association
24350 Orchard Lake Road, Suite 105
Farmington Hills, MI 48336
(248) 473-9070

National Association of Social Workers: Michigan Chapter
741 North Cedar Street, Suite 100
Lansing, MI 48906
(517) 487-1548

Minnesota

Minnesota Psychological Association
1711 West County Road B, Suite 310N
Roseville, MN 55113-4036
(651) 697-0440

National Association of Social Workers: Minnesota Chapter
1885 University Avenue West, Suite 340
St. Paul, MN 55104
(651) 293-1935

Mississippi

Mississippi Psychological Association
P.O. Box 1120
Jackson, MS 39215-1120
(601) 321-4629

National Association of Social Workers: Mississippi Chapter
P.O. Box 4228
Jackson, MS 39216
(601) 981-8359

Missouri

Missouri Psychological Association
211 East Capitol
Jefferson City, MO 65101-2989
(573) 634-8852

National Association of Social Workers: Missouri Chapter
Parkade Center, Suite 138
601 Business Loop 70 West
Columbia, MO 65203
(573) 874-6140

Montana

Montana Psychological Association
P.O. Box 50247
Billings, MT 59105
(406) 252-2559

National Association of Social Workers: Montana Chapter
25 South Ewing, Suite 406
Helena, MT 59601
(406) 449-6208

Nebraska

Nebraska Psychological Association
1044 H Street
Lincoln, NE 68508-1896
(402) 475-0709

National Association of Social Workers: Nebraska Chapter
P.O. Box 83732
Lincoln, NE 68501
(402) 477-7344

Nevada

Nevada State Psychological Association
PMB184
10580 North McCarren Boulevard, Suite 115
Reno, NV 89503-1896
(800) 840-6772

National Association of Social Workers: Nevada Chapter
1555 East Flamingo Road, Suite 158
Las Vegas, NV 89119
(702) 791-5872

New Hampshire

New Hampshire Psychological Association
P.O. Box 1205
Concord, NH 03302-1205
(603) 225-9925

National Association of Social Workers: New Hampshire Chapter
c/o New Hampshire Association of the Blind
25 Walker Street
Concord, NH 03301
(603) 226-7135

New Jersey

New Jersey Psychological Association
349 East Northfield Road, Suite 211
Livingston, NJ 07039-4806
(973) 535-9888

National Association of Social Workers: New Jersey Chapter
2 Quarterbridge Plaza
Hamilton, NJ 08619
(609) 584-5686

New Mexico

New Mexico Psychological Association
2501 San Pedro NE, Suite 113
Albuquerque, NM 87110
(505) 883-7376

National Association of Social Workers: New Mexico Chapter
1503 University Boulevard NE
Albuquerque, NM 87102
(505) 247-2336

New York

New York Psychological Association
Six Executive Park Drive
Albany, NY 12203
(518) 437-1040

National Association of Social Workers: New York City Chapter
50 Broadway, 10th Floor
New York, NY 10004
(212) 668-0050

National Association of Social Workers: New York State Chapter
188 Washington Avenue
Albany, NY 12210
(518) 463-4741

North Carolina

North Carolina Psychological Association
1004 Dresser Court, Suite 106
Raleigh, NC 27609-7353
(919) 872-1005

National Association of Social Workers: North Carolina Chapter
P.O. Box 27582
Raleigh, NC 27611-7581
(919) 828-9650

North Dakota

North Dakota Psychological Association
419 East Brandon Drive
Bismarck, ND 58501-0410
(701) 223-9045

National Association of Social Workers: North Dakota Chapter
P.O. Box 1775
Bismarck, ND 58502-1775
(701) 223-4161

Ohio

Ohio Psychological Association
400 East Town Street, Suite G20
Columbus, OH 43215-1599
(614) 224-0034

National Association of Social Workers: Ohio Chapter
118 East Main Street, Suite 3 West
Columbus, OH 43215
(614) 461-4484

Oklahoma

Oklahoma Psychological Association
601 West I-44 Service Road, Suite C
Oklahoma City, OK 73118-6032
(405) 879-0069

National Association of Social Workers: Oklahoma Chapter
116 East Sheridan, Suite 210
Oklahoma City, OK 73104-2419
(405) 239-7017

Oregon

Oregon Psychological Association
147 Southeast 102nd Street
Portland, OR 97216
(503) 253-9155

National Association of Social Workers: Oregon Chapter
7688 Southwest Capitol Highway
Portland, OR 97219
(503) 452-8420

Pennsylvania

Pennsylvania Psychological Association
416 Forster Street
Harrisburg, PA 17102-1714
(717) 232-3817

National Association of Social Workers: Pennsylvania Chapter
1337 North Front Street
Harrisburg, PA 17102
(717) 758-3588

Rhode Island

Rhode Island Psychological Association
500 Prospect Street
Pawtucket, RI 02860-6260
(401) 728-5570

National Association of Social Workers: Rhode Island Chapter
260 West Exchange Street
Providence, RI 02903
(401) 274-4940

South Carolina

South Carolina Psychological Association
P.O. Box 5207
Columbia, SC 29250-5207
(803) 771-6050

National Association of Social Workers: South Carolina Chapter
P.O. Box 5008
Columbia, SC 29250
(803) 256-8406

South Dakota

South Dakota Psychological Association
P.O. Box 460
Sioux Falls, SD 57101-0460
(605) 373-8969

National Association of Social Workers: South Dakota Chapter
1000 North West Avenue, #360
Spearfish, SD 57783
(605) 339-9104

Tennessee

Tennessee Psychological Association
P.O. Box 281296
Memphis, TN 38168
(901) 372-1015

National Association of Social Workers: Tennessee Chapter
1808 West End Avenue, Suite 805
Nashville, TN 37203
(615) 321-5095

Texas

Texas Psychological Association
1011 Meredith Drive, Suite 4
Austin, TX 78748
(512) 280-4099

National Association of Social Workers: Texas Chapter
810 West Eleventh Street
Austin, TX 78701
(512) 474-1454

Utah

Utah Psychological Association
275 East South Temple, Suite 112
Salt Lake City, UT 84111
(801) 359-5646

National Association of Social Workers: Utah Chapter
University of Utah GSSW, Room 229
359 South 1500 East
Salt Lake City, UT 84112-0260
(800) 888-6279

Vermont

Vermont Psychological Association
P.O. Box 1017
Montpelier, VT 05601-1017
(802) 229-5227

National Association of Social Workers: Vermont Chapter
P.O. Box 1348
Montpelier, VT 05601
(802) 223-1713

Virginia

Virginia Psychological Association
109 Amherst Street
Winchester, VA 22601-4182
(540) 667-5544

National Association of Social Workers: Virginia Chapter
1506 Staples Mill Road
Richmond, VA 23230
(804) 204-1339

Washington

Washington State Psychological Association
P.O. Box 2016
Edmonds, WA 98020-2016
(425) 712-1852

National Association of Social Workers: Washington Chapter
2366 Eastlake Avenue East, Room 302
Seattle, WA 98102
(206) 322-4344

West Virginia

West Virginia Psychological Association
P.O. Box 58058
Charleston, WV 25358
(304) 345-5805

National Association of Social Workers: West Virginia Chapter
1608 Virginia Street East
Charleston, WV 25311
(304) 345-6279

Wisconsin

Wisconsin Psychological Association
121 South Hancock Street
Madison, WI 53703-3461
(608) 251-1450

National Association of Social Workers: Wisconsin Chapter
16 North Carroll Street, Suite 220
Madison, WI 53703
(608) 257-6334

Wyoming

Wyoming Psychological Association
P.O. Box 1191
Laramie, WY 82073-1191
(307) 745-3167

National Association of Social Workers: Wyoming Chapter
P.O. Box 701
Cheyenne, WY 82003
(307) 634-2118

Other Related Resources

AARP Webplace: Model Programs for Grandparents Raising
Grandchildren
www.aarp.org/confacts/grandparents/modelprgs.html

American Association for Marriage and Family Therapy
www.aamft.org

American Counseling Association
5999 Stevenson Avenue
Alexandria, VA 22304
(703) 823-9800

Association for Gay, Lesbian, and Bisexual Issues in Counseling
www.aglbic.org

Contract with Your Stepchild
(sample of contract between stepparent and stepchild, helping each
to understand what to expect from the relationship)
www.stepparenting.about.com/parenting

Dovetail Institute for Interfaith Family Resources
(a nonprofit organization that supports both Christian and Jewish
exploration of issues concerning interfaith family building in a
nonjudgmental manner)
www.dovetailinstitute.org

Family Diversity Projects Inc.
(for issues related to all types of family diversity)
Peggy Gillespie and Gigi Kaesner
P.O. Box 1209
Amherst, MA 01004-1209
(413) 256-0502

The Foundation for Grandparenting
www.grandparenting.org

Gay and Lesbian Adoption
www.adopting.org/gaystate.html

GrandsPlace
(devoted to grandparents and other special people raising children)
www.grandsplace.com

HealthPLACE: Blending Families
(helping children to adjust to new families)
www.highmark.com/healthplace/blend.html

Is There a Recipe for Blending Families?
(Practical Parenting supports parents and professionals)
www.practicalparent.org.uk/blend.htm

Lesbian and Gay Aging Issues Network
www.asaging.org/lgain.html

Is there a recipe for "blending families"?
(dedicated to helping parents, grandparents, stepparents, single
parents, and gay and lesbian families blend)
www.family2000.org.uk/blended.htm

Momazons
(national organization and referral network by and for lesbians
choosing children)
www.momazons.org

The Patchwork Family
(a wellness approach to strengthening families with adopted
children and stepchildren)
www.patchworkfamily.com

The "Stepfamily" Bookstore
(dedicated to providing reading resources for those striving to build
healthy, happy blended families)
www.concentric.net/~Lismith/STEP.HTM

Stepfamily Life Can Be Hell
www.abrandes.com

The Waiting Game
www.stepparenting.about.com

When You're Not the Brady Bunch
(examines the establishment of effective coparenting agreements)
www.parentsplace.com

Zero to Three—It's Not the Same the Second Time Around:
Grandparents Raising Grandchildren
www.zerotothree.org/parent.html?Load=2nd_time.html

Index